D. W. Winnicott

Home Is Where We Start From

Essays by a Psychoanalyst

Compiled and Edited by
Clare Winnicott,
Ray Shepherd,
Madeleine Davis

PENGUIN BOOKS

Penguin Books Ltd, Harmondsworth, Middlesex, England
Viking Penguin Inc., 40 West 23rd Street, New York, New York 10010, U.S.A.
Penguin Books Australia Ltd, Ringwood, Victoria, Australia
Penguin Books Canada Ltd, 2801 John Street, Markham, Ontario, Canada L3R 1B4
Penguin Books (N.Z.) Ltd, 182–190 Wairau Road, Auckland 10, New Zealand

First published by W. W. Norton & Company 1986
Published in Pelican Books 1986
Reprinted 1987

Made and printed in Great Britain by
Richard Clay Ltd, Bungay, Suffolk
Typeset in Monophoto Plantin

Contents

Part 3   Reflections on Society

Home is where one starts from. As we grow older
The world becomes stranger, the pattern more
    complicated
Of dead and living. Not the intense moment
Isolated, with no before and after,
But a lifetime burning in every moment

T. S. ELIOT
'East Coker', *Four Quartets*

Preface

When Donald Winnicott died in 1971 he left behind some eighty papers which had never been published. Along with these were many papers published in books and journals that have now become difficult to obtain. It is from these two groups that the bulk of the present volume is drawn, though as the sections took shape a few papers from Winnicott's own books were added to round them off (details of original publication can be found in the Acknowledgements at the end of the text).

Winnicott himself was planning to make further collections of his work for publication; but had he been able to do so, it is unlikely that his selection and arrangement of material would have been the same as ours. The selection is therefore our responsibility, and we gratefully acknowledge the help of Robert Tod in the initial stages. The editing of the un-published papers has purposely been kept to a minimum, even though we feel that Winnicott would probably have polished them up before presenting them to the public.

Our principle in selecting the papers for this volume has been the breadth of their interest and concern. They nearly all began as talks and lectures, for Winnicott enjoyed re-sponding to invitations to speak to a wide variety of people. The result is a book in which ideas and themes are sometimes repeated, but which we hope will show the depth of his conviction that the structure of society reflects the nature of the individual and of the family, as well as his own keen sense of responsibility for the particular society in which he lived. We also hope that it will give pleasure to the reader – something that he especially would have wished.

Clare Winnicott
Ray Shepherd
Madeleine Davis
London, February 1983

Acknowledgements

The publishers are grateful for the opportunity to reproduce material already published in the following books and journals:

'The Concept of a Healthy Individual' in *Towards Community Mental Health*, edited by J. D. Sutherland (London: Tavistock Publications, 1971); '*Sum*, I Am' in *Mathematics Teaching* (March 1984); 'The Value of Depression' in *British Journal of Psychiatric Social Work* (vol. 7, no. 3, 1964); 'Delinquency as a Sign of Hope' in the *Prison Service Journal* (vol. 7, no. 27, April 1968); 'The Mother's Contribution to Society' in *The Child and the Family* (London: Tavistock Publications, 1957) and also partly in the Introduction to *The Child, the Family and the Outside World* (London: Penguin Books, 1984); 'Children Learning' in *The Human Family and God* (London: Christian Teamwork Institute of Education, 1968); 'Adolescent Immaturity' in *Proceedings of the British Student Health Association* (1969), also in *Playing and Reality* (London: Tavistock Publications, 1971; New York: Basic Books, 1971; Harmondsworth: Penguin Books, 1985) and also partly in *Pediatrics* (USA) (vol. 44. no. 5, 1 November 1969); 'Thinking and the Unconscious' in the *Liberal Magazine* (March 1945); 'The Price of Disregarding Psychoanalytic Research' in *The Price of Mental Health: Report of the National Association for Mental Health Annual Conference* (London, 1965); 'Freedom' (in French) in

Nouvelle Revue de Psychanalyse (no. 30, 1984); 'Some Thoughts on the Meaning of the Word "Democracy"' in *Human Relations* (vol. 3, no. 2, June 1950) and also in *The Family and Individual Development* (London: Tavistock Publications, 1965, 1968).

The following papers are published for the first time in this volume:

'Psychoanalysis and Science: Friends or Relations?' (1961); 'Living Creatively' (1970); 'The Concept of the False Self' (1964); 'Aggression, Guilt and Reparation' (1960); 'Varieties of Psychotherapy' (1961); 'Cure' (1970); 'The Child in the Family Group' (1966); 'This Feminism' (1964); 'The Pill and the Moon' (1969); 'Discussion of War Aims' (1940); 'Berlin Walls' (1969); 'The Place of the Monarchy' (1970).

The Editors acknowledge with gratitude help from The Squiggle Foundation in producing the transcript of 'The Pill and the Moon', and from Dr Colin Morley with the mechanics of the index.

Psychoanalysis and Science: Friends or Relations?

A talk given to the Oxford University Scientific Society, 19 May 1961

Psychoanalysis is a method for treating psychiatrically ill people by psychological means, that is to say, without apparatus, drugs or hypnotism. It was evolved by Freud at the turn of the century, when hypnotism was being used to remove symptoms. Freud became dissatisfied by his own results and by those of his colleagues, and, moreover, he found that if he removed a symptom by hypnotism, he was no further in his understanding of the patient; so he adapted the hypnotism setting to one in which he was working with the patient, being on equal terms with him, and letting time bring what it might. The patient came daily at a set time, and there was no hurry to remove symptoms, a more important thing having emerged: to enable the patient to reveal himself to himself. In this way Freud also became informed, and he used the information obtained both to interpret the patient to himself and also for the purpose of gradually building up a new science, the science that we now call psychoanalysis. It could be called dynamic psychology.

So *psychoanalysis* is a term that refers specifically to a method and to a growing body of theory, theory that concerns the emotional development of the human individual. It is an applied science based on a science.

You will observe that I have slipped in the word 'science', giving away my own view that Freud did really start up a new science, an extension of physiology, one which concerns human personality, character, emotion and endeavour. This is my thesis.

But what is meant by science? This is a question that has often been asked, and answered.

About scientists I would say this: that when a gap in knowledge turns up, the scientist does not flee to a supernatural explanation. This would imply panic, fear of the unknown, an other-than-scientific attitude. For the scientist every gap in understanding provides an exciting challenge. Ignorance is held, and a research programme is devised. The stimulus for the work done is the existence of the gap. The scientist can afford to wait and to be ignorant. This means he has some sort of faith – not a faith in this or in that, but a faith, or a capacity for faith. 'I don't know. Well, OK! Perhaps one day I will. Perhaps not. Then perhaps someone else will.'

For the scientist the formulation of questions is almost the whole thing. The answers, when found, only lead on to other questions. The nightmare of the scientist is the idea of complete knowledge. He shudders to think of such a thing. Compare this with the certainty that belongs to religion, and you will see how different science is from religion. Religion replaces doubt with certainty. Science holds an infinity of doubt, and implies a faith. Faith in what? Perhaps in nothing; just a capacity to have faith; or if there must be faith in something, then faith in the inexorable laws that govern phenomena.

Psychoanalysis goes on where physiology leaves off. It extends the scientific territory to cover the phenomena of human personality, human feeling and human conflict. It claims, therefore, that human nature can be examined; and where ignorance is exposed, psychoanalysis can afford to wait and need not indulge in a flight to superstitious formulations. One of the main contributions of science is the halt that it calls to hurry, fuss and bother; it gives time for a breather. We may play our game of bowls and beat the Spaniards too.

I invite you to keep separate in your minds the science and the applied science. Day by day as practitioners in applied science, we meet the needs of our patients or of normal people who come for analysis; often we succeed, often we fail. That we fail can no more be helped than it can be helped that an aeroplane develops a crystallization of metal and disintegrates at an awkward moment. Applied science is not science. When I do an analysis, this is not science. But I depend on the science when I do work that could not have been done before Freud.

Freud was able to develop the theory on which psychoanalysis is based very far indeed in his own lifetime, and this theory is usually called metapsychology (on the analogy of metaphysics). He studied psychoneurosis, but gradually extended his inquiries to cover the more deeply disturbed patient, the schizophrenic and the manic-depressive. Much of what is now known about the psychology of schizophrenia and manic-depressive psychosis has been the result of work done by Freud and by those who have continued to use the method of investigation and treatment invented by him.

I am at a disadvantage here because I do not know you, I don't know what you know, and don't know whether you easily agree with what I have said or whether you have quite other sorts of ideas that you consider I have neglected. Probably you will want me to describe psychoanalysis and I will try to do so. There is, of course, much too much to be said if anything is said at all.

First you must have an idea of the general scheme of the emotional development of human beings. Then you must know about the tensions that are inherent in life, and the ways that are employed for dealing with such tensions. And then you must know about the breakdown of the normal defences and the establishment of second and third lines of defence, in other words, of the organization of illness as a way of carrying on in face of the failure of ordinary defences. Underlying the tensions are the instincts, the body functions that operate orgiastically.

Of course, part of the individual's defence against intolerable anxiety is always the environmental provision. The setting for life evolves, normally, along with the individual, so that the dependence of the infant gradually develops into the independence of the older child and the autonomy of the adult. All this is very complex and has been worked out in great detail.

It is possible to classify illness in terms of environmental breakdown. More interesting, however, is the study of illness in terms of the organization of defences in the individual. Each of these lines of approach teaches us about the life of ordinary normal people: one teaches us about society, and the other teaches us about the personal human tensions which are the concern of philosophers and artists and of religion. In other words, psychoanalysis has deeply affected our way of looking at life, and there is much more to come from psycho-analysis than has yet been brought across to the study of society and of ordinary people. In the meantime psycho-analysis continues to be a method of investigation which has no parallel or rival. But a lot of people don't like it, or the idea of it, and so there are comparatively few practising an-alysts in this country, and they nearly all live in London.

What is the main thing that psychoanalysis tells us about people? It tells us about the unconscious, about the deep and hidden life of each human individual, that which has roots in the real and imaginative life of earliest childhood. At the beginning these two things, the real and the imaginative life, are one and the same thing, because the infant at the beginning does not perceive objectively, but lives in a sub-jective state, being the creator of all. Gradually, in health the infant becomes able to perceive a world that is a not-me world, and to attain this state the infant must be cared for well enough at the time of absolute dependence.

Through the dream and dreaming people know about their own unconscious, and dreams represent a bridge between conscious life and unconscious phenomena. Freud's *The Interpretation of Dreams* (1900) remains the cornerstone of his contribution.

Of course, often dreams only come up because of the

special circumstances of the consultation. Psychoanalysis provides extra special circumstances, and the most important dreams in psychoanalysis indirectly or directly concern the analyst. In the 'transference' comes the material for interpretation in a long series of samples of the repressed unconscious revealing defences against anxiety.

Psychoanalysis has a special relation to science in that it begins to show the nature of science in these ways:

1. The origin of a scientist.
2. The way that scientific research deals with anxiety about fantasy and reality (subjective–objective).
3. The scientific method of the *creative impulse*, appearing as a *new question*, i.e. dependent on knowledge of existing knowledge.

The new question comes because of an idea about its solution. The sequence of the scientific method could be seen as: (a) institution of expectations; (b) acceptance of proof or relative proof; (c) new questions arising out of relative failure.

What about statistics? Is this science? Statistics can be used to prove that some answer to a question is right, but whose question is it, and whose answer?

It is sometimes argued that the psychoanalyst is a psychiatrist biased in favour of the method because of his own analysis. If this is true in some cases, it cannot be helped; it does not prove that psychoanalytic theory is wrong. To practise psychoanalysis the analyst must have experienced it, unless he has the genius of Freud.

As in hypnotism, amazing things happen in psychoanalysis, but not in an amazing way. They happen bit by bit, and what comes comes because it is acceptable to the patient. I cannot give spectacular psychoanalytic material. It would be easier to find instances of dramatic change in child psychiatry; but in psychoanalysis proper, patient and analyst just plod away day after day until the end of the treatment.

For example, a man comes to analysis because he cannot marry. Gradually he reveals himself, and he finds (1) healthy heterosexual trends interfered with by (2) female identification as a flight from homosexuality and (3) incest taboo too thoroughly accepted; so he is free to have any girl because no one stands for the mother of the Oedipus complex. Gradually this resolves, and he marries, but now has to start to build a family. The next problem is to sort out his relationship to his brother, whose existence he had denied. In the process he discovers the depth of his love as a boy for his father.

He then finds the hate of his father-figure more manageable and becomes an easier person at work. Another new aim develops: to explore deeper or earlier aspects of love of his mother, including the roots of the self in primitive impulse. Result: not just a cure of symptoms, but a more widely based personality richer in feeling and more tolerant of others because more sure of himself. This already reflects itself in his handling of his infants and his ability to see the value of his very well-chosen wife. His work develops at the same time, with more drive and originality.

Statistics could not show these changes.

Part 1

Health and Illness

The Concept of
a Healthy Individual

*A talk given to the Royal Medico-Psychological
Association, Psychotherapy and Social
Psychiatry Section, 8 March 1967*

Preliminaries

We use the words 'normal' and 'healthy' when we talk about
people, and we probably know what we mean. From time to
time we may profit from trying to state what we mean, at risk
of saying what is obvious and at risk of finding we do not
know the answer. In any case our standpoint moves on with
the decades, so that a statement that suited us in the forties
might seem to serve us badly in the sixties.

I shall not start off with quotations from those authors
who have dealt with this same subject. Let me say at once
that I have derived most of my concepts from those of
Freud.

I hope that I shall not fall into the error of thinking that an
individual can be assessed apart from his or her place in
society. Individual maturity implies a movement towards
independence, but there is no such thing as independence. It
would be unhealthy for an individual to be so withdrawn as
to feel independent and invulnerable. If such a person is
alive, then there is dependence indeed! Dependence 'on
mental nurse or family.

Nevertheless, I shall study the concept of the health of the
individual, because social health is dependent on individual
health, society being but a massive reduplication of persons.
Society cannot get further than the common denominator of

individual health, and indeed cannot get so far, since society needs must carry its unhealthy members.

Maturity at Age

In terms of development it can be said that health means maturity according to the maturity that belongs to the age of the individual. Premature ego development or premature self-awareness is no more healthy than is delayed awareness. The tendency towards maturation is part of that which is inherited. In a complex way (which has received much study) development, especially at the beginning, depends on a good-enough environmental provision. A good-enough environment can be said to be that which facilitates the various individual inherited tendencies so that development takes place according to these inherited tendencies. Inheritance and the environment are each external factors if we speak in terms of the emotional development of the individual person, that is to say, of psychomorphology. (I have wondered whether this term could be used instead of the clumsy use of the word 'psychology', prefixed by the word 'dynamic'.)

It can usefully be postulated that the good-enough environment starts with a high degree of adaptation to individual infant needs. Usually the mother is able to provide this because of the special state she is in, which I have called primary maternal preoccupation. Other names have been given to this state, but I am using my own descriptive term. Adaptation decreases according to the baby's growing need to experience reactions to frustration. In health the mother is able to delay her function of failing to adapt, till the baby has become able to react with anger rather than be traumatized by her failures. Trauma means the breaking of the continuity of the line of the individual's existence. It is only on a continuity of existing that the sense of self, of feeling real, and of being, can eventually be established as a feature of the individual personality.

Infant–Mother Interrelationships

It is at the beginning, when the baby is living in a subjective world, that health cannot be described in terms of the individual alone. Later it becomes possible for us to think of a healthy child in an unhealthy environment, but these words make no sense at the beginning, till the baby has become able to make an objective assessment of actuality, and has become able to be clear about the not-me as distinct from the me, and between the shared *actual* and the phenomena of personal psychical reality, and has something of an internal environment.

I am referring to the two-way process in which the infant lives in a subjective world and the mother adapts in order to give each infant a basic ration of the *experience of omnipotence*. A living relationship is involved, essentially.

The Facilitating Environment

The facilitating environment and its progressive adjustments adaptive to individual needs could be isolated for study as a part of the study of health. Included would be the paternal functions supplementing the mother's functions, and the function of the family with its more and more (as the child becomes older) complex manner of introducing the Reality Principle while at the same time giving back the child to the child. Here, however, my aim is not to study the evolution of the environment.

Erotogenic Zones

In the first half century of Freud any statement of health would need to be made in terms of the stage of id-establishment according to the successive predominance of erotogenic zones. This still has validity. The hierarchy is well known – starting with oral primacy, followed by anal and urethral primacies, and then followed by the phallic or 'swank' stage (the one that is so difficult for girl toddlers), and finally by the genital phase (three to five years) in which the *fantasy* includes all that belongs to adult sex. We are happy when a child fits in with this blueprint for growth.

Then in health the child reaches the characteristics of the latency period, in which there is no forward movement of id-positions and there is but sparse backing to id-impulse from the endocrine apparatus. The concept of health here is associated with the existence of a period of teachability, and in this period the sexes tend rather naturally to segregate themselves. These matters have to be mentioned, because it is healthy to be six at six and ten at ten.

Then comes puberty, usually announced by a prepubertal phase in which a homosexual tendency may perhaps manifest itself. By the age of fourteen the boy or girl who has not stepped over into puberty may be inherently, and *in health*, thrown into a state of confusion and doubt. The word 'doldrums' has been usefully applied here. Let me emphasize that it is not illness when a mid-puberty boy or girl flounders.

Puberty comes both as a relief and as an immensely disturbing phenomenon, one that we are only just beginning to be able to understand a little. At the present time boys and girls at puberty are able to experience adolescence as a period of growth in company with others in the same state; and the difficult task of sorting out what belongs to health and what belongs to illness in adolescence belongs to the post-war era in particular. The problems are, of course, not new.

One can only ask for those who are engaged in this task to put the emphasis on the solution of the theoretical problems rather than on the solution of the actual problems of the adolescents, who may, in spite of the inconvenience of their symptomatology, be best able to find their own salvation. The passage of time has significance here. The adolescent is not to be cured as if ill. I think this is an important part of the statement of health. This is not to deny that there can be illness during this age period when adolescence is due.

Some adolescents suffer greatly, so that it is almost cruel to offer no help. At fourteen they are commonly suicidal, and theirs is the task of tolerating the interaction of several disparate phenomena – their own immaturity, their own puberty changes, their own idea of what life is about, and their own ideals and aspirations; add to this their personal disillusionment about the world of grown-ups – which for them seems to be essentially a world of compromise, of false values, and of infinite distraction from the main theme. As they leave this stage, adolescent boys and girls are beginning to feel real, to have a sense of *self* and of *being*. This is health. From being comes doing, but there can be no *do* before *be*, and this is their message to us.

We need not encourage adolescents who have personal difficulties, and who tend to be defiant while still dependent, and indeed they do not need encouragement. We remember that late adolescence is the age of exciting achievement in adventure, so that the emergence of a boy or girl from adolescence to the beginnings of an identification with parenthood and with responsible society is something that is good to watch. No one would claim that the word 'health' is synonymous with the word 'ease'. This is specially true in the area of conflict between society and its adolescent contingent.

If we proceed we begin to use a different language. This section started in terms of id-drives and ends up in terms of ego psychology. It is a great help to the individual when puberty can bring a potential for male potency and for the equivalent in girls, that is to say, when full genitality is already a feature, having been reached in the reality of play at the age preceding the latency period. Nevertheless, boys and girls at puberty are not deceived into thinking that instinctual drives are all, and in fact they are essentially concerned with being, with being somewhere, with feeling real, and with achieving a degree of object constancy. They need to be able to ride the instincts rather than be torn to pieces by them.

Maturity or health in terms of the achievement of full genitality takes on a special form when the adolescent changes over into the adult who may become a parent. It is convenient when a boy who wishes to be like his father is able to dream heterosexually and to perform in full genital power; also when a girl, who wishes to be like mother, is able to dream heterosexually and experience genital orgasm in sexual intercourse. The test is: can sexual experience join up with liking and with the wider meanings of the word 'love'?

Ill health in these respects is a nuisance, and inhibitions can be destructive and cruel in their operation. Impotence can hurt more than rape. Nevertheless, we do not feel contented nowadays with a statement of health in terms of id-positions. It is easier to describe the developmental process in terms of id-function than in terms of the ego and its complex evolution, yet the second method cannot be avoided. We must attempt to do this.

Where there is immaturity in the instinctual life, then there is danger of ill health in the individual, in personality or character or behaviour; but one must be careful here to understand that sex can operate as a part-function so that, although sex may *seem* to be working well, potency and its female equivalent can be found to deplete, instead of enrich, the individual. But we are not easily taken in by these things, since we are not looking at the individual according to behaviour and surface phenomena. We are prepared to examine the personality structure and the relationship of the individual to society and to ideals.

Perhaps at one time psychoanalysts did tend *to think of health in terms of the absence of psychoneurotic disorder*, but this is no longer true. We now need more subtle criteria. We need not throw away what we used formerly when we now think in terms of freedom within the personality, of capacity for trust and faith, of matters of reliability and object constancy, of freedom from self-deception, and also of something that has to do with richness rather than poverty as a quality of personal psychical reality.

The Individual and Society

If we assume reasonable achievement in terms of instinct capacity, then we see new tasks for the relatively healthy person. There is, for instance, his or her relationship to society – an extension of the family. Let us say that in health a man or woman is able *to reach towards an identification with society without too great a loss of individual or personal impulse.* There must, of course, be loss in the sense of control of personal impulse, but the extreme of identification with society with total loss of sense of self and self-importance is not normal at all.

If it is clear, then, that we are not contented with the idea of health as a simple absence of psychoneurotic disorder – that is, of disturbances relative to the progression of id-positions towards full genitality, and the organization of defence in respect of anxiety in interpersonal relationships – we can say in this context that health is not ease. The life of a healthy individual is characterized by fears, conflicting feelings, doubts, frustrations, as much as by the positive features. The main thing is that the man or woman feels he or she *is living his or her own life*, taking responsibility for action or inaction, and able to take credit for success and blame for failure. In one language it can be said that the individual has emerged from dependence to independence, or to autonomy.

The thing that was unsatisfactory about the statement of health in terms of id-positions was the absence of ego psychology. A look at the ego takes us right back to the pregenital, preverbal stages of individual development, and to the environmental provision: adaptation geared to the primitive needs that are characteristic of earliest infancy.

At this point I tend to think in terms of HOLDING. This goes for the physical holding of the intra-uterine life, and gradually widens in scope to mean the whole of the adaptive care of the infant, including handling. In the end this concept can be extended to include the function of the family, and it leads on to the idea of the casework that is at the basis of social work. Holding can be done well by someone who has no intellectual knowledge of what is going on in the individual; what is needed is a capacity to identify, to know what the baby is feeling like.

In an environment that holds the baby well enough, the baby is able to make *personal development according to the inherited tendencies*. The result is a continuity of existence that becomes a sense of existing, a sense of self, and eventually results in autonomy.

Development in Early Stages

Now I wish to look at what is going on in the early stages of personality development. Here the key word is *integration*, which covers almost all the developmental tasks. Integration carries the baby through to unit status, to the personal pronoun 'I', to the number one; this makes possible I AM, which makes sense of I DO.

It will be appreciated that I am now looking in three directions at once. I am looking at infant care. Also I look at schizoid illness. In addition, I am seeking a way of stating what life can be about for healthy children and adults. In parentheses, I would say that it is a characteristic of health that the adult does not stop developing emotionally.

I will take three examples. In the case of a baby, *integration* is a process, one that has its own pace and increasing complexity. In schizoid disorder, the phenomenon of *disintegration* is a feature, especially the fear of disintegration and the pathological organization of defences in the individual designed to give warning of disintegration. (Insanity is usually not a regression, which has an element of trust in it; it is rather a sophisticated arrangement of defences whose object is to prevent a repetition of disintegration.) Integration as a process of the kind that features in infant life reappears in the psychoanalysis of the borderline case.

In adult life, integration is enjoyed along with the ever-extending meaning of the term right up to and including integrity. Disintegration, in resting and in relaxation and in dreaming, can be allowed by the healthy person, and the pain associated with it accepted, especially because relaxation is associated with creativity, so that it is out of the *unintegrated* state that the creative impulse appears and reappears. Organized defence against disintegration robs the individual of the precondition for the creative impulse and therefore prevents creative living.[1]

The Psychosomatic Partnership

A subsidiary task in infant development is that of psychosomatic indwelling (leaving the intellect out for the moment). Much of the physical part of infant care – holding, handling, bathing, feeding, and so on – is designed to facilitate the baby's achievement of a psyche–soma that lives and works in harmony with itself.

In psychiatry again, it is a feature of schizophrenia that there is only a loose connection between the psyche (or whatever it may be called) and the body and its functions. The psyche may even be absent from the soma for a considerable period of time, or may be projected.

In health the use of the body and all its functions is one of the enjoyable things, and this applies especially to children and to adolescents. So here again is a relationship between schizoid disorder and health. It is distressing that healthy

1. It is thought by some, as in Balint's paper (in *Problems of Human Pleasure and Behaviour*, 1952) discussing Khan, that much of the pleasure in the experience of art in one form or another arises from the nearness to unintegration to which the artist's creation may safely lead the audience or viewer. So where the artist's achievement is potentially great, failure near the point of achievement may cause great pain to the audience by bringing them close to disintegration or the memory of disintegration, and leaving them there. The appreciation of art thus keeps people on a knife-edge, because achievement is so close to painful failure. This experience must be reckoned part of health.

persons may have to live in deformed or diseased or old bodies, or may be starving or in great pain.[2]

Object-relating

Relating to objects can be looked at in the same way as psychosomatic coexistence and the wider issue of integration. Object-relating is something that the maturational process drives the baby to achieve, but cannot happen securely unless the world is presented to the baby well enough. The adapting mother presents the world in such a way that the baby starts with a ration of the *experience of omnipotence*, this being the proper foundation for his or her later coming to terms with the Reality Principle. A paradox is involved here, in that in this initial phase the baby creates the object, but the object is already there, else he would not have created it. The paradox has to be accepted, not resolved.

Now let us carry this over to the fields of mental illness and to adult health. In schizoid illness, object-relating goes wrong; the patient relates to a subjective world or fails to relate to any object outside the self. Omnipotence is asserted by means of delusions. The patient is withdrawn, out of contact, bemused, isolated, unreal, deaf, inaccessible, invulnerable, and so on.

In health a great deal of life has to do with various kinds of object-relating, and with a 'to-and-fro' process between relating to external objects and relating to internal ones. In full fruition this is a matter of interpersonal relationships, but the residues of creative relating are not lost, and this makes every aspect of object-relating exciting.

2. Here belongs another complication – the intellect, or the part of the mind that may become split off, and be exploited at great cost in terms of healthy living. A good intellect is no doubt a wonderful thing, so special to human beings, but there is no need for the intellect to be too closely linked in our minds with the idea of health. Study of the place of the intellect relative to the area I am discussing is an important subject, consideration of which would be out of place.

Health here includes the idea of tingling life and the magic of intimacy. All these things go together and add up to a sense of feeling real and of being, and of the experiences feeding back into the personal psychical reality, enriching it, and giving it scope. The consequence is that the healthy person's inner world is related to the outer or actual world and yet is personal and capable of an aliveness of its own. Introjective and projective identifications are constantly taking place. It follows that loss and ill fortune (and illness, as I have said) may be more terrible for the healthy than for those who are psychologically immature or distorted. Health must be allowed to carry its own risks.

Recapitulation

At this stage of the argument we must burden ourselves with a consideration of our terms of reference. We need to decide whether to confine our consideration of the meaning of health to those who are healthy from the beginning, or to extend it to cover those who carry a germ of ill health and yet manage to 'make it' in the sense of reaching in the end a state of health that did not come easily and naturally. I feel we must include this latter category. I will very briefly describe what I mean.

Two Kinds of Person

I find it useful to divide the world of people into two classes. There are those who were never 'let down' as babies and who are to that extent candidates for the enjoyment of life and of living. There are also those who did suffer traumatic experience of the kind that results from environmental letdown, and who must carry with them all their lives the memories (or the material for memories) of the state they were in at moments of disaster. These are candidates for lives of storm and stress and perhaps illness.

We recognize the existence of those who lost grip of the

tendency towards healthy development, and whose defences
are organized in rigidity, the rigidity being itself a guarantee
against forward movement. We cannot extend our meaning
of the word 'health' to cover this state of affairs.

There is a middle group, however. In a fuller exposition of
the psychomorphology of health, we would include those
who carry round with them experiences of unthinkable or
archaic anxiety, and who are defended more or less successfully against remembering such anxiety, but who
nevertheless use any opportunity that turns up to become ill
and have a breakdown in order to approach that which was
unthinkably terrible. The breakdown only seldom leads to a
therapeutic result, but the positive element in the breakdown
must be acknowledged. Sometimes the breakdown does lead
to a kind of cure, and then the word 'health' turns up again.

There seems to be a tendency towards healthy development
that persists even here, and if these people in my second
category can manage to hitch on to this tendency towards
development, even if late, they may yet make good. We can
then include these in among the healthy. Healthy by hook or
by crook.

Flight to Sanity

We need now to remind ourselves that a flight to sanity is not
health. Health is tolerant of ill health; in fact, health gains
much from being in touch with ill health in all its aspects,
especially the ill health called schizoid, and with dependence.

In between the two extremes of the first or lucky group
and the second or unlucky group (in respect of early environmental provision), there is a big proportion of all
persons who successfully hide a relative need for breakdown,
but who do not actually break down unless existing environmental features trigger it off. These may take the form
of a new version of the trauma, or it may be that a reliable
human being has raised hopes.

So we ask ourselves the question: how wide a spectrum of these people who are making good in spite of what they carry round with them (genes, early let-downs and unfortunate experiences) do we include among those who are healthy? We have to take into consideration the fact that in this group are many uncomfortable people whose anxiety propels them to exceptional achievement. They may be difficult to live with, but they push the world forward in some area of science, art, philosophy, religion or politics. I do not have to decide the answer, but I do have to be prepared for the legitimate question: what about the world's geniuses?

True and False

There is a special case of this awkward category, in which potential breakdown dominates the scene, that does not, perhaps, give us so much trouble. (But nothing in human affairs is clear-cut, and who shall say where health stops and ill health takes over?) I refer to those people who have unconsciously needed to organize a false-self front to cope with the world, this false front being a defence designed to protect the true self. (The true self has been traumatized and it must never be found and wounded again.) Society is easily taken in by the false-self organization, and has to pay heavily for this. The false self, from our point of view here, though a successful defence, is not an aspect of health. It merges into the Kleinian concept of a manic defence – where there is a depression but this depression is denied, by unconscious process of course, so that the symptoms of depression appear as their opposites (up for down, light for heavy, white or luminous for dark, liveliness for deadness, excitement for indifference, and so on).

This is not health, but it has a healthy aspect in terms of holidays, and it also has a happy link with health, in that for ageing or old people the quickness and liveliness of the young is a perpetual, and surely legitimate, counter to depression. Seriousness has its link, in health, with the heavy responsibilities that come with age, responsibilities that the young wot not of, usually.

Here I need to mention the subject of *depression* itself – a price to pay for integration. It will not be possible for me to repeat here what I have written on the subject of the value of depression, or rather the health that is inherent in the capacity to be depressed, the depressed mood being near to the ability to feel responsible, to feel guilty, to feel grief, and to feel the full joy when things go well. It is true, however, that depression, however terrible, is to be respected as evidence of personal integration.

In ill health there are complicating destructive forces that when inside the individual favour suicide and when outside carry liability to delusions of persecution. I am not suggesting that these elements are part of health. Nevertheless, in a study of health it is necessary to include the seriousness akin to depression that belongs to individuals who have grown up in the sense of having become whole. It is in such persons that we can find richness and potential in a personality.

Omissions

I must omit the localized subject of the antisocial tendency. This is related to deprivation, that is to say, to a good era that came to an end at a phase in the child's growth when the child could know, but could not cope with, its results.

This is not the place to write about aggression. Let me say, however, that in the community it is the ill members who are compelled by unconscious motives to go to war and to attack as a defence against delusions of persecution, or else to destroy the world, a world that annihilated them, each one of them separately, in their infancy.

Life's Purpose

I want finally to look at the life that the healthy person is able to live. What is life about? I do not need to know the answer, but we can agree that it is more nearly about BEING than about sex. Lorelei said: 'Kissing is all very well but a diamond bracelet lasts for ever.'[3] Being and feeling real belong essentially to health, and it is only if we can take being for granted that we can get on to the more positive things. I contend that this is not just a value judgement, but that there is a link between individual emotional health and a sense of feeling real. No doubt the vast majority of people take feeling real for granted, but at what cost? To what extent are they denying a fact, namely, that there could be a danger for them of feeling unreal, of feeling possessed, of feeling they are not themselves, of falling for ever, of having no orientation, of being detached from their bodies, of being annihilated, of being nothing, nowhere? Health is not associated with *denial* of anything.

The Three Lives

My last word must be about the three lives that healthy people live.

1. The life in the world, with interpersonal relationships as the key even to making use of the non-human environment.

2. The life of the personal (sometimes called inner) psychical reality. This is where one person is richer than another, and deeper, and more interesting when creative. It includes dreams (or what dream material springs out of).

With these two you are familiar, and it is well known that either may be exploited as a defence: the extrovert needs to find fantasy in living; and the introvert may become self-sufficient, invulnerable, isolated and socially useless. But there is another area for human health to enjoy, one that is not easily referred to in terms of psychoanalytic theory:

3. The area of cultural experience.

3. Anita Loos, *Gentlemen Prefer Blondes*, New York, Brentano, 1935.

Cultural experience starts as play, and leads on to the whole area of man's inheritance, including the arts, the myths of history, the slow march of philosophical thought and the mysteries of mathematics, and of group management and of religion.

Where do we place this third life of cultural experience? I think it cannot be placed in the inner or personal psychical reality, because it is not a dream – it is a part of shared reality. But it cannot be said to be part of external relationships, because it is dominated by dream. Also, of the three lives, it is the most variable; in some anxious, restless people it has practically no representation, whereas in others this is the important part of human existence, where animals do not even start. For into this area come not only play and a sense of humour, but also all the accumulated culture of the past five to ten thousand years. In this area the good intellect can operate. It is all a by-product of health.

I have tried to work out where cultural experience is located, and I have tentatively made this formulation: that it starts *in the potential space between a child and the mother when experience has produced in the child a high degree of confidence in the mother*, that she will not fail to be there if suddenly needed.

Here I find I join up with Fred Plaut,[4] who used the word 'trust' here as the key to the establishment of this area of healthy experience.

Culture and Separation

In this way health can be shown to have a relationship with living, with inner wealth, and, in a different way, with the capacity to have cultural experience.

In other words, in health there is no separation, because in the space–time area between the child and the mother, the child (and so the adult) lives creatively, making use of

4. F. Plaut, 'Reflections About Not Being Able to Imagine', *Journal of Analytical Psychology*, vol. 11, 1966.

the materials that are available – a piece of wood or a late Beethoven quartet.

This is a development of the concept of transitional phenomena.

There is very much more that could be said about health, but I hope I have succeeded in giving the idea that I think a human being is unique. Ethology is not enough. Human beings have animal instincts and functions, and at times they look very much like animals. Perhaps lions are more noble, monkeys are more nimble, gazelles more graceful, snakes more sinuous, fishes more prolific, and birds more lucky because they are able to fly, but human beings are quite a thing on their own, and when they are healthy enough, they do have cultural experiences superior to those of any animal (except perhaps whales and their relatives).

It is human beings who are likely to destroy the world. If so, we can perhaps die in the last atomic explosion knowing that this is not health but fear; it is part of the failure of healthy people and healthy society to carry its ill members.

Summary

What I hope I have done is to:

1. Use the concept of health as absence of psychoneurotic illness.

2. Link health with maturation ending with maturity.

3. Point out the importance of maturational processes that concern the ego rather than those related to a consideration of id-positions in the hierarchy of erotogenic zones.

4. Link these ego processes with infant care, schizoid illness and adult health, using in passing the concepts of

  (a) integration

  (b) the psychosomatic partnership

  (c) object-relating

as examples of what obtains in the total scene.

5. Point out that we have to decide how far to include, and

whether to include, those who reach to health in spite of handicaps.

6. Name the three areas in which human beings live, and suggest that it is a matter of health that some lives are valuable and effective, that some personalities are rich and creative, and that for some experience in the cultural area is the most important bonus that health brings.

7. Lastly, indicate not only that society depends for its health on the health of its members, but also that its patterns are those of its members reduplicated. In this way democracy (in one meaning of the word) is an indication of health because it arises naturally out of the family, which is in itself a construct for which healthy individuals are responsible.

Living Creatively

*An amalgamation of two drafts of a talk
prepared for the Progressive League, 1970*

Definition of Creativity

Whatever definition we arrive at, it must include the idea that life is worth living or not, according to whether creativity is or is not a part of an individual person's living experience.

To be creative a person must exist and have a feeling of existing, not in conscious awareness, but as a basic place to operate from.

Creativity is then the doing that arises out of being. It indicates that he who is, is alive. Impulse may be at rest, but when the word 'doing' becomes appropriate, then already there is creativity. *Not able to do.*

It is possible to show that in some people at certain times the activities that indicate that the person is alive are simply reactions to stimulus. A whole life may be built on the pattern of reacting to stimuli. Withdraw the stimuli and the individual has no life. But in the extreme of such a case, the word 'being' has no relevance. In order to be and to have the feeling that one *is*, one must have a predominance of impulse-doing over reactive-doing.

These things are not just a matter of the will and of the arrangement and rearrangement of life. The basic patterns are laid down in the process of emotional growth, and near the beginning are the factors that have the greatest influence. Most people must be presumed to be somewhere in the middle between the two extremes, and it is in this midway area that there is opportunity for us to affect our own patterns; and it is this opportunity which we feel we have that makes this sort of discussion interesting, not merely an academic exercise. (Also, we are considering what we can do as parents and educators.)

Creativity, then, is the retention throughout life of something that belongs properly to infant experience: the ability to create the world. For the baby this is not difficult, because if the mother is able to adapt to the baby's needs, the baby has no initial appreciation of the fact that the world was there before he or she was conceived or conceived of. The Reality Principle is the fact of the existence of the world whether the baby creates it or not.

The Reality Principle is just too bad, but by the time the little child is called upon to say 'ta', big developments have taken place and the child has acquired genetically determined mental mechanisms for coping with this insult. For the Reality Principle is an insult.

I am ready to describe some of these mental mechanisms. Given good-enough environmental conditions, the individual child (who became you and me) found ways of absorbing the insult. Compliance, at one extreme, simplifies the relationship with other people who, of course, have their own needs to attend to, their own omnipotence to cater for. At the other extreme the child retains omnipotence in the guise of being creative and having a personal view of everything.

To give a crude illustration: if a mother has eight children, there are eight mothers. This is not simply because of the fact that the mother was different in her attitude to each of the eight. If she could have been exactly the same with each (and I know this is absurd, for she is not a machine), each child would have had his and her own mother seen through individual eyes.

By an extremely complex process of growth genetically determined, and the interaction of the individual's growth with external factors that tend to be positively facilitating or unadaptive and reaction-producing, the child that became you or me found itself equipped with some capacity to see everything in a fresh way, to be creative in every detail of living.

I could look up creativity in *The Oxford English Dictionary*, and I could do research on all that has been written on the subject in philosophy and psychology, and then I could serve it all up on a dish. Even this could be garnished in such a way that you would exclaim: 'How original!' Personally, I am unable to follow this plan. I have this need to talk as though no one had ever examined the subject before, and of course this can make my words ridiculous. But I think you can see in this my own need to make sure I am not buried by my theme. It would kill me to work out the concordance of creativity references. Evidently I must be always fighting to *feel* creative, and this has the disadvantage that if I am describing a simple word like 'love', I must start from scratch. (Perhaps that's the right place to start from.) But I will return to this theme when I get to the distinction between creative living and creative art.

I have now looked up the word 'create' in a dictionary, and I find: 'bring into existence'. A creation can be 'a production of the human mind'. It is not certain that creativity is a word at all acceptable to the erudite. By creative living I mean not getting killed or annihilated all the time by compliance or by reacting to the world that impinges; I mean seeing everything afresh all the time. I refer to apperception as opposed to perception.

Origins of Creativity

Perhaps I have shown what I believe to be the origin of creativity. There has to be a double statement. Creativity belongs to being alive – so that unless at rest, the person is reaching out in some way so that if an object is in the way there can be a relationship. But this is only one half. The other half belongs to the idea that reaching out physically or mentally has no meaning except for a being who is there to be. A baby born with nearly no brain may reach out and find and use an object, but there has been no experience of creative living. Also, the normal baby needs to grow in complexity and to become an established exister in order to be experiencing reaching out and finding an object as a creative act.

So I come back to the maxim: Be before Do. Be has to develop behind Do. Then eventually the child rides even the instincts without loss of sense of self. The origin, therefore, is the individual's genetically determined tendency to be alive and to stay alive and to relate to objects that get in the way when the moments come for reaching out, even for the moon.

Maintaining Creativity

For the individual who is not too distorted by faulty introduction to the world, there is considerable scope for fostering this most desirable attribute. It is true, as you will certainly point out to me, that a great deal of living can be a chore. Someone has to do the chores. It is difficult to discuss clearly, because there are some who even find chores useful; perhaps the fact that not much intelligence is needed for scrubbing a floor leaves welcome opportunity for a split-off area of imaginative experience. But there is also the matter of cross-identifications, which I will deal with later. A woman may be scrubbing a floor and not be bored because she is enjoying making a muddy mess vicariously, through identification with her horrid child who, in moments of creative living, brings in the garden mud and tramples it in. He works on the assumption that mothers love cleaning up floors, and this is his potency, appropriate to his horrid age. (People refer to this as phase-adequate. That makes it sound quite good I always think!)

Or a man may be as near bored as possible working on a conveyor-belt, but when he thinks of the money, he is also thinking of that improvement he hopes to make to the kitchen sink or he is already watching Southampton surprisingly beat Manchester City on his TV, only half paid for.

The fact is that people must not take jobs that they find stifling – or if they cannot avoid this, they must organize their weekends so as to feed the imagination, even at the worst moments of boring routine. It has been said that it is easier to keep the imaginative life going in a truly boring routine than in an area of somewhat interesting work. It must be remembered, too, that the work may be very interesting to someone else who is using it for creative living, but who does not allow anyone else to use personal discretion.

Somewhere in the scheme of things there can be room for everyone to live creatively. This involves retaining something personal, perhaps secret, that is unmistakably yourself. If nothing else, try breathing, something no one can do *for* you. Or perhaps you are yourself when writing to your friend, or sending letters to *The Times* and *New Society*, presumably to be read by someone before being thrown away.

Creative Living and Artistic Creation

In mentioning letter writing, I am getting near to another subject which I must not leave aside. I must make clear the distinction between creative living and being artistically creative.

In creative living you or I find that everything we do strengthens the feeling that we are alive, that we are ourselves. One can look at a tree (not necessarily at a picture) and look creatively. If you have ever had a depression phase of the schizoid sort (and most have), you will know this in the negative. How often I have been told: 'There is a laburnum outside my window and the sun is out and I know intellectually that it must be a grand sight, for those who can see it. But for me this morning (Monday) there is no meaning in it. I cannot feel it. It makes me acutely aware of not being myself real.'

Although allied to creative living, the active creations of

letter writers, writers, poets, artists, sculptors, architects, musicians, are different. You will agree that if someone is engaged in artistic creation, we hope he or she can call on some special talent. But for creative living we need no special talent. This is a universal need, and a universal experience, and even the bedridden, withdrawn schizophrenic may be living creatively in a secret mental activity, and therefore in a sense happy. Unhappy is a you or a me who, over a phase, is conscious of the lack of what is essential to the human being, much more important than eating or than physical survival. If we had time, there is something to be said here about the anxiety that is a drive behind the artist's brand of creativity.

Creative Living in Marriage

There seems to be a need for a discussion based on the fact that in one or both partners in a marriage there is quite frequently a feeling of initiative ebbing. Something appears here which is a common experience, although there must be much variation in the degree to which this feeling is important relative to all the other things about life which could be said. Here and now I must take it for granted that *not all married couples feel that they can be creative as well as married.* One or the other of the two finds himself or herself involved in a process which could end in one living in a world which is really created by the other. In the extreme this must be very uncomfortable, but I suppose that in the majority of cases it does not reach an extreme state, although it is always latent and may from time to time appear in an acute form. The whole problem may, for instance, be hidden under a couple of decades of child-rearing and emerge as a mid-life crisis.

There is probably a rather simple way of talking about this problem if one starts at the surface. I know two people who have been married a long time and brought up quite a large family. In the first summer holiday of their marriage, after they had spent a week together, the man said: 'Now I'm going off to have a week's sailing.' His wife said: 'Well, I like travelling so I am packing my bag.' Their friends put up their hands and said: 'I can't see much future for that marriage!' However, the prognostications were too gloomy and these people have made a very successful marriage, and one of the most important things about it is that the man gets his sailing week in which he increases his skill and enjoys his speciality, whereas his wife has taken her suitcase all over Europe. They have a lot to tell each other in the remaining fifty-odd weeks and find it a help in their relationship that they walk away from each other for half of every summer holiday.

There are many who would not like this. There is no rule about human beings which applies universally. Nevertheless, this instance could illustrate how two people are not afraid to leave each other, they have much to gain, and if they are afraid to leave each other, they are liable to get bored with each other. This boredom could be a result of clamping down on creative living, which essentially arises from the individual, not from the partnership, although a partner may inspire creativity.

If we look at practically any family that is a going concern, we will find the equivalent of this arrangement that I have described in the case of these two people. I need not fill out the details; how the wife plays the violin and the man spends an evening a week in a pub sipping shandy with a few friends. With human beings there is an infinite variety in normality or health. If we decide to talk about *difficulties*, it is certain that we shall find ourselves describing patterns which people find themselves involved in, and which they find themselves boringly repeating, and which indicate that there is something wrong somewhere. There is a compulsive element in it all, and this compulsive element has fear somewhere a long way at the back of it. There are many who are unable to be creative because they are caught up in compulsions which belong to something to do with their own past history. I think that it is only to those who are relatively happy in this respect, that is, who are not driven by compulsions, that I can talk with ease about being hampered in marriage. To people who are bothered because a relationship seems to be stifling them, one can say but little. There is no useful advice one can give and one cannot be doing everybody's therapy.

Between the two extremes – those who feel they retain creative living in marriage and those who are hampered in this respect by marriage – there is surely some kind of borderline; and on this borderline very many of us happen to be situated. We are *happy enough*, and can be creative, but we do realize that there is inherently some kind of a clash between the personal impulse and the compromises that belong to any kind of relationship that has reliable features. In other words, we are once more talking about the Reality Principle, and eventually, as we pursue our argument, shall find ourselves going over again some aspect of the individual's attempt to accept external reality without too much loss of personal impulse. This is one of several basic troubles that belong to human nature, and it is at the early stages of one's own personal emotional development that the basis of one's own capacity in this respect is being laid down.

One could say that we often talk about the successful marriage in terms of how many children there are, or in terms of the friendship which the two partners are able to build up. We can easily be glib about these matters, and I know you do not want me to keep to that which is facile and superficial. If we talk about sex, which, after all, must be given a central place in a discussion on marriage, we shall find a most amazing quantity of distress everywhere. It would be quite a good axiom, I suggest, that it is not common to find married people who feel that in their sexual life they each live creatively. A great deal has been written about all this, and perhaps it is the psychoanalyst's misfortune that he knows more about these difficulties and the distress that goes with them than most people do. It is not possible for the psychoanalyst to maintain the illusion that people get married and live happily ever afterwards, at any rate in their sexual life. When two people are in love and they are young there

can be a time, and it can be a prolonged one, in which their
sexual relationship is a creative experience for each. This
indeed is health and we are glad when young people unself-
consciously experience this at first hand. I think it is very
wrong if we advertise to young people the idea that it is
common for such a state of affairs to last for a long period
after marriage. Someone said (only, I am afraid, facetiously):
'There are two kinds of marriage; in one the girl knows she
has married the wrong man on the way up to the altar, and in
the other she knows it on the way back.' But there is no
reason to be funny about it really. The trouble is when we set
out to give young people the idea that marriage is a prolonged
love affair. But I would hate to do the opposite and to sell
disillusionment to young people, to make it a business to see
that young people know everything and have no illusions. If
one *has been happy*, one can bear distress. It is the same when
we say that a baby cannot be weaned unless he or she has had
the breast, or breast equivalent. There is no disillusionment
(acceptance of the Reality Principle) except on a basis of
illusion. It does give people a terrible sense of failure when
they find that such an important thing as sexual experience is
becoming more and more a creative experience for only one
of the couple. It can work well sometimes when sex starts off
badly, and gradually the two people achieve some kind of
compromise, or give and take, so that there is eventually
some creative experience on both sides.

One has to say that mutual sexuality is healthy and a great
help, but it would be wrong to assume that the only solution
to life's problems is in mutual sex. We need to pay attention
to what is latent, when sex, as well as being an enriching
phenomenon, is also an ever-recurring therapy.

Here I want to remind you of the special mental mechanisms of projection and introjection: I mean the functions
of identifying oneself with others and others with oneself. As
you would expect, there are those who cannot use these
mechanisms, and there are those who can if they will, and
there are those who do so compulsively whether they want to

or not. In plain English, I refer to being able to stand in other people's shoes, and to matters of sympathy and empathy.

Obviously, when two people live together with a close and publicly announced tie as in marriage, they have full scope for each living through the other. In health this can be exploited or not, according to circumstances. But some couples find themselves awkwardly handing over roles to each other, whereas in other cases there is fluidity and flexibility of all degrees. Clearly it is convenient if a woman can hand over to the man the male part of the physical sex act, and the same the other way round. However, there is not only acting; there is also the imagination, and *imaginatively* there is surely no part of life that cannot be handed over or taken over.

With this in our minds, we can look at the special case of creativity. There is not much in it when it comes to an examination of the sex function: who is more creative, a father or a mother? I would not like to say. We can leave this question aside. But right in this area of *actual* functioning, it has to be remembered that a baby may be *conceived* uncreatively – that is, without being *conceived of*, without having been arrived at as an idea in the mind. On the other hand, a baby may start up just at the right moment when it is wanted by both parties. In *Who's Afraid of Virginia Woolf?* Edward Albee studies the fate of a baby that is conceived of, but without taking flesh. What a remarkable study both in play and film!

But I want to drag myself away from this matter of actual sex and actual babies, because everything that we do can be done creatively or uncreatively. I want to take up again the theme of the origins of the individual's capacity to live creatively.

More about the Origins of Creative Living

It is the old, old story. What we are like depends very much on where we have arrived in our emotional development, or how far we were given opportunity for that part of growth that has to do with the early stages of object-relating, and I want to talk about this.

I know I shall be saying: happy is he or she who is being creative all the time in personal life as well as through life partners, children, friends, etc. There is nothing that is outside this philosophical territory.

I can look at a clock and only see the time; maybe I do not even see that, but only notice the shapes on the dial; or I see nothing. On the other hand, I may be seeing clocks potentially, and then I allow myself to hallucinate a clock, doing so because I have evidence that an actual clock is there to be seen, so when I perceive the actual clock I have already been through a complex process that originated in me. So when I see the clock I create it, and when I see the time I create time too. Every moment I have my little experience of omnipotence, before I hand this uncomfortable function over to God.

There is some antilogic here. Logic takes the form at one point of unlogic. I can't help this – this is actual. I want to go into this matter.

The infant becomes ready to find a world of objects and ideas, and, at the pace of growth of this aspect of the baby, the mother is presenting the world to the baby. In this way, by her high degree of adaptation at the beginning, the mother enables the baby to experience omnipotence, to actually find what he creates, to create and link this up with what is actual. The nett result is that each baby starts up with a new creation of the world. And on the seventh day we hope that he is pleased and takes a rest. This is when things go reasonably well, as, in fact, they usually do; but someone has to be there if that which is created is to be realized, actual. If no one is there to do this, then, in the extreme, the child is autistic – creative into space – and boringly compliant in relationships (childhood schizophrenia).

Then the Reality Principle may be gradually introduced, and the child who has known omnipotence experiences the limitations that the world imposes. But by that time he or she is able to live vicariously, to use projection and introjection mechanisms, to let the other person be the manager sometimes, and to hand over omnipotence. Eventually the individual human being relinquishes being the wheel, or the whole gearbox, and adopts the more comfortable position of a cog. Help me to write a humanist hymn:

> O! to be a cog
> O! to stand collectively
> O! to work harmoniously with others
> O! to be married without losing the
>   *idea* of being the creator of the world.

The human individual who does not start off with an experience of omnipotence has no chance to be a cog, but must go on pushing round omnipotence and creativeness and control, like trying to sell unwanted shares in a bogus company.

In my writings I have made a lot of the concept of the transitional object: something your child may be clutching on to just now, perhaps a bit of cloth that once belonged to the cot-cover, or was a blanket or mother's hair-ribbon. It is a first symbol, and it stands for confidence in the union of baby and mother based on the experience of the mother's reliability and capacity to know what the baby needs through identification with the baby. I have said this object was created by the baby; we know we will never challenge this, although we also know it was there before the baby created it. (It may even have been created in the same way by a sibling.)

Not 'Ask and it shall be given,' so much as 'Reach out and it shall be there for you to have, to use, to waste.' This is the beginning. It must be lost in the process of the introduction of the actual world, of the Reality Principle, but in health we devise ways and means for recapturing the feeling of meaningfulness that comes from creative living. The symptom of uncreative living is the feeling that nothing means anything, of futility, I couldn't care less.

We are now in a position to look at creative living, and in so doing to use a consistent theory. The theory allows us to see some of the reason why the subject of creative living is inherently difficult. We can look at the generality or at the details of which creative living is composed.

It will be understood that I am trying to get to a layer that is somewhat deep if not actually fundamental. I know that one way of cooking sausages is to look up the exact directions in Mrs Beeton (or Clement Freud on Sundays) and another way is to take some sausages and somehow to cook sausages for the first time ever. The result may be the same on any one occasion, but it is more pleasant to live with the creative cook, even if sometimes there is a disaster or the taste is funny and one suspects the worst. The thing I am trying to say is that *for the cook* the two experiences are different: the slavish one who complies gets nothing from the experience except an increase in the feeling of dependence on authority, while the original one feels more real, and surprises herself (or himself) by what turns up in the mind in the course of the act of cooking. When we are surprised at ourselves, we are being creative, and we find we can trust our own unexpected originality. We shall not mind if those who consume the sausages fail to notice the surprising thing that was in the cooking of them, or if they do not show gustatory appreciation.

I believe there is nothing that has to be done that cannot be done creatively, if the person is creative or has that capacity. But if someone is all the time threatened by creative extinction, then either the boring compliance has to be endured or else originality has to be piled on until the sausages come out looking like something out of this world or tasting like a garbage bin.

I believe it is true, as I have already indicated, that however poor the individual's equipment, experience can be creative and can be felt to be exciting in the sense that there is always something new and unexpected in the air. Of course, if the person is highly individual and talented, their drawing may be worth £20,000, but for those who are not Picassos, it would be slavish imitation and non-creative to draw like Picasso. To draw like Picasso one has to be Picasso – else it is uncreative. The hangers-on in a coterie are by definition compliant and boring except so far as they were seeking something and needed Picasso's courage for support in being original.

The fact is that what we create is already there, but the creativeness lies in the way we get at perception through conception and apperception. So when I look at the clock, as I must do now, I create a clock, but I am careful not to see clocks except just where I already know there is one. Please do not turn down this piece of absurd unlogic – but look at it and use it.

To help matters, may I say that if it is getting dark, and if I am exhausted, or a bit schizoid anyway, I may see clocks where there are none. I may see something on the wall over there and even read the time on its dial, and you could tell me that it's just a shadow thrown on a wall by someone's head.

For some, the chance of being found to be mad, hallucinated, makes them stick to sanity, and to objectivity of the kind that could be called shared actuality. Also, others allow themselves to pretend too well that what they imagine is actual and able to be shared.

We can allow all kinds of people to live with us in the world, but we need the others to be objective if we are to enjoy our creativeness and take risks and follow up our impulses with the creative ideas that go with them.

Some children have to grow up in an atmosphere of glorious creative living which belongs to a parent or a nurse, but not to the children. This stifles them and they cease to be. Or they develop a technique of withdrawal.

There is a whole vast subject of the provision of opportunity for children to live their own lives both at home and at school, and it is an axiom that children who easily feel they exist in their own right are the very ones who are easy to manage. These are the ones who are not insulted right, left and centre by the operation of the Reality Principle.

If we are formally joined with partners, we may allow all manner and all degrees (as I have said) of projections and introjections, and a wife may enjoy her husband's enjoyment of his work or a husband enjoy his wife's experiences with the frying pan. So in that way marriage – formal union – widens our scope for creative living. You may be creative by proxy while you are doing a chore that gets done more quickly if you can do it as it says on the label of the bottle.

I wonder how you are getting on with these ideas that I have written down, and that I have read. The first thing is that I cannot make you creative by talking at you. I would do better by listening than by talking. If you have not had or have lost the capacity for surprising yourself in your living experiences, then I cannot give any help by talking, and you would be difficult to help by psychotherapy. But it is important that we know of others (especially children for whom we may be responsible) that experience of creative living is always more important for the individual than doing well.

What I do want to make clear is that creative living involves, in every detail of its experience, a philosophical dilemma – because, in fact, in our sanity we only create what we find. Even in the arts we cannot be creative into the blue unless we are having a solo experience in a mental hospital or in the asylum of our own autism. Being creative in art form or in philosophy depends very much on the study of all that exists already, and the study of the milieu is a clue to the understanding and appreciation of every artist. But the creative approach makes the artist feel real and significant, even when what he does is a failure from the point of view of the public, although the public remains as necessary a part of his equipment as his talents, his training and his tools.

So my claim is that in so far as we are fairly healthy personally, we do not have to live in a world created by our marriage partner and our marriage partner does not have to live in ours. Each of us has his or her own private world, and, moreover, we learn to share experiences by use of all degrees of cross-identifications. Where we are bringing up children or starting babies off as creative individuals in a world of actual facts, we do have to be uncreative and compliant and adaptive; but, on the whole, we get round this and find it does not kill us because of our identification with these new people who need us if they too are to achieve creative living.

Sum, I Am

A talk given to the Association of Teachers of Mathematics during their Easter Conference at Whitelands, Putney, London, 17 April 1968

Certainly it would be good here and now for me to stick to my last, which is child psychiatry and the theory of the emotional development of the child that belongs to psychoanalysis and therefore ultimately to Freud. In my own job *I do know something*, and I have expertise and I have accumulated experience. In the areas of mathematics and of teaching I am a *greenhorn*. Your newest student knows more than I do. Certainly I would not have accepted Mr Tahta's and your invitation, except that in his initial letter he seemed to know that I belong to an alien speciality, and that he could only expect from me a comment on the ecology of the particular garden that I happen to cultivate.

I am even frightened of my title '*Sum*, I am', lest it be thought that I am a classics scholar or a master of etymology. Pressed for a title some months ago, I thought, 'Well, I shall be talking about the stage of *I am* in individual development, and so it might be legitimate to link this with the Latin word *sum*.' 'You catch the paronomasia . . .?' (That's Calverley, but not to think I'm erudite either.)

My job is definitely to be myself. What bit of myself can I give you, and how can I give you a bit without seeming to lack wholeness? I must assume that you can allow me a wholeness and some degree of that form of maturation that we call integration, and I must choose to show you just one

or two of the elements that go to make up the unity which is
ME.

Already I feel encouraged, because I know that these
matters that are the concern of the student of the human
personality are also the concern of the mathematician, and,
in fact, mathematics is a disembodied version of the human
personality.

In a word, when I say that the central feature in human
development is the arrival and secure maintenance of the
stage of I AM, I know this is also a statement of the central
fact of arithmetic, or (as one could say) of sums.

You will already have perceived that by nature and by
training and by practice I am a person who thinks developmentally. When I see a boy or a girl at a desk adding
and subtracting and struggling with the multiplication table,
I see a person who already has a long history in terms of the
developmental process, and I know that there may be developmental deficiencies, developmental distortions, or
distortions organized to deal with deficiencies that have to be
accepted, or that there may be a certain precariousness in
respect of developments that seem to have been achieved. I
see the development towards independence and ever-new
meanings to the concept of wholeness that may or may not
become a fact in that child's future if the child lives. Also, I
am all the time aware of dependence and the way that the
environment, originally all-important, continues to have significance, and will have significance even when the individual
reaches towards independence by means of an identification
with environmental features, as when a child grows up and
marries and brings up a new generation of children, or begins
to take part in social life and in the maintenance of the social
structure.

This is the aspect of me that you may be able to use,
because if we stick to our lasts, *you* cannot be expected to be
concerned with developmental processes as *I* need to be if I
am to do my work at all, let alone effectually.

It is difficult for us to remember how modern is the concept of a human individual. The struggle to reach to this concept is reflected, perhaps, in the early Hebrew name for God. Monotheism seems to be closely linked to the name I AM. I am that I am. (*Cogito, ergo sum* is different: *sum* here means I have a *sense* of existing as a person, that in my mind I feel my existence has been proved. But we are concerned here with an unselfconscious state of being, apart from intellectual exercises in self-awareness.) Does not this name (I AM) given to God reflect the danger that the individual feels he or she is in on reaching the state of individual being? If I am, then I have gathered together this and that and have claimed it as me, and I have repudiated everything else; in repudiating the not-me I have, so to speak, insulted the world, and I must expect to be attacked. So when people first came to the concept of individuality, they quickly put it up in the sky and gave it a voice that only a Moses could hear.

This accurately portrays the anxiety that is inherent in the arrival of every human being who gets there at the I AM stage. You can see it at work in the game you played on the beach, 'I'm the King of the Castle'. Immediately comes defence against expected attack: 'You're the dirty rascal!' or 'Get down, you dirty rascal.' Horace had a version of this children's game:

> *Rex erit qui recte faciet;*
> *Qui non faciet, non erit.*[1]

Of course, this is a sophisticated version of the I AM stage, with I AM being allowed only to the King.

One wonders how there can have been sums before monotheism. What I mean is, the word 'unit' means nothing except in so far as the human being is a unit. In another context we would be discussing the use of the personal first pronoun 'I', which I believe generally (ME or I) comes first of the pronouns in childhood speech. However, the issue is

1. From *The Oxford Dictionary of Nursery Rhymes*, edited by Iona and Peter Opie, Oxford University Press, 1951.

not clear here, because spoken words may be long preceded by the understanding of language, and highly complex mental processes belong to the era that goes before verbalization.

You will easily see what I am getting at: the idea that arithmetic starts with the concept of one, and that this derives and must derive in every developing child from the unit self, a state that represents an achievement of growth, a state indeed that may never be achieved.

I must now interrupt myself in order to deal with an immense complication. What is to be done with the split-off intellectual process? Higher mathematics can function here apart from the individual's achievement or non-achievement of unit status. In other fields we recognize the same problem. Take, for example, the judge in the probate division who dies without having made (presumably without having been able to make?) a will; or the philosopher who doesn't know the date or the day of the week; or the physicist of great fame, like the late Master of Trinity, Cambridge, who might be seen walking with one foot on the pavement and the other in the gutter (hence the necessity for Hobson's Brook between the pavement and the road in Trumpington Street, or so I fondly believed when I was a schoolboy at The Leys).

Let me look at this in terms of individual development. (By the way, I have stated this at length, and I find it difficult to discuss it briefly except in caricature.) Here is a baby getting hungry, and beginning to be ready for something. If the feed comes, then okay. But if the coming of the feed is delayed more than X minutes, then when it comes it is meaningless for the baby. Now the question arises, how abruptly does the moment arrive after which the feed is meaningless?

Now take two babies: one has the equipment which will eventually show on test as giving him or her a high I Q, and the other is endowed below average. The well-endowed baby soon gets to know from 'noises off' that a feed is being prepared. Without verbalization the baby talks to himself and says: 'Those noises allow me to predict a feed, so, hang on! and the chances are all will be well.' The poorly endowed baby is more at the mercy of the mother's capacity for adaptation, and has a more exact figure for the symbol *X*.

Can you see from this that the intellect helps in the toleration of frustration? From this one can go on to see that a mother can exploit a baby's intellectual functions in order to get free from the tie that comes from the baby's dependence. All this is quite normal, but if you give the baby an intellectual equipment that is well above average, the baby and the mother may collude in exploitation of the intellect which becomes split off – split off, that is from the psyche of psychosomatic existence and living.

Add to this an element of difficulty in the psychosomatic field, then the baby begins to develop a false self in terms of a life in the split-off mind, the true self being psychosomatic, hidden, and perhaps lost; so that while higher mathematics gets a boost, the child fails to know what to do with one penny.

A patient who helped to teach me this easily learned 'The Pied Piper of Hamelin' at five or six years, but she was increasingly unsure of herself, so that eventually she came to treatment in order to lose her split-off intellectual capacity (of which her parents were proud) and to find her true self. At the age of six or seven she dictated to her nurse for the family magazine a story of a child, obviously herself, who was doing very well at school and who gradually became mentally defective. She was over fifty when she got free in the course of her analysis.

You will understand that I think the intellect is a fine thing, but in my work I can see how it can be exploited, and in a descriptive account of the personality I need to take into account the amazing achievements of the split-off intellect without losing sight of the individual's psychosomatic existence.

In the old days – a hundred years ago – people talked of mind and body. To get away from the dominance of the split-off intellect, they had to postulate a soul. Now it is possible to start with the psyche of the psyche–soma and from this basis for personality structure to proceed to the concept of the split-off intellect, which at its extreme, and in a person with rich intellectual endowment in terms of grey matter, can function brilliantly without much reference to the human being. But it is the human being who, by an accumulation of experiences duly assimilated, may achieve wisdom. The intellect only knows how to talk about wisdom. You might quote: 'How can he get wisdom whose talk is of bullocks?' (Ecclesiasticus 38:25).

So, from the point of view that I am adopting here, there is no limit to addition and subtraction, to division and multiplication, in the split-off intellect, except that which may be determined by the computer, here happening to be the human brain, which is no doubt very much like the computers that you invent and use as part of your speciality. But there is a limit to the sums that an individual can feel identified with, and this limit belongs to the stage of personality development which the individual has reached and can maintain.

(We have started on a big theme. The trouble is I don't know where to stop. There is so much to be said.)

Let us look at division.

In the split-off intellect, division presents no difficulties. In fact, there are no difficulties in this area except in terms of computers and programming. This is not life, it is split off from life. But let us consider how does the individual reach to division? On the basis of unit status, the achievement which is basic to health in the emotional development of every human being, the unit personality can afford to identify with wider units – say, the family or the home or the house. *Now* the unit personality is part of a wider concept of wholeness. And soon will be part of a social life of an ever-widening kind; and of political matters; and (in the case of a very few persons here and there) of something that can be called world-citizenship.

The basis of such divisibility is the unit self, perhaps

handed over (because of fear of attack) to God. So we come
back to monotheism, and the achievement of a meaning for
one, alone, only; how quickly the one is broken up into three,
the trinity! Three, the simplest possible family number.

When you teach sums, you have to teach the children as
they come, and you will certainly recognize the three types:

1. Those who easily start with *one*.
2. Those who have not achieved unit status and for whom
one means nothing.
3. Those who manipulate concepts and who are held back
by banal considerations of pounds, shillings and pence.

You will feel like starting these last children off on the slide-
rule and differential calculus. Why not ask them to *guess*
rather than to *calculate*, thus using their personal computers?
I don't see why, in arithmetic, there is so much emphasis *on
the accurate answer*. What about the fun of guessing? Or of
playing around with ingenious methods? I suppose you have
given thought to all these matters in your theory of teaching
method.

What I think you must not expect is that a child who has
not reached unit status can enjoy bits and pieces. These are
frightening to such a child and represent chaos. So what do
you do? In such cases you leave arithmetic aside and try to
provide the stable environment that may (even though be-
latedly and irksomely) enable some degree of personal
integration to take place in the child who has this immaturity.
Perhaps such a child will be devoted to a mouse. Well, this is
good arithmetic, even if smelly. In terms of the mouse, the
child can get to the wholeness that cannot be achieved in the
self. Also, the mouse may die. This is very important. There
is no death except of a totality. Put the other way round, the
wholeness of personal integration brings with it the *possibility*
and indeed the *certainty of death*; and with the acceptance of
death there can come a great relief, relief from fear of the
alternatives, such as disintegration, or ghosts – that is the
lingering on of spirit phenomena after the death of the

somatic half of the psychosomatic partnership. Healthy children are rather better at death than adults, I would say.

Perhaps I may usefully refer to one more item in the developmental statement. This is the interaction of personal processes and environmental provision. This is sometimes referred to as the balance between nature and nurture. In thinking on this particular problem, most people tend to take sides, but there is no need to be in favour of the one or the other.

The new human baby inherits tendencies towards growth and development, including the qualitative aspects of development. One can say that at one year the baby will have three words, at sixteen months will probably be starting to walk, and at two years will be speaking. These are developmental nodes (Greenacre) and it is highly convenient when a child reaches each developmental stage at the natural time, within the time span of the node.

This is simple to state, but it leaves out the important fact of dependence. Dependence on the environmental provision is at first near-absolute, and this rapidly becomes relative, and the general tendency is towards independence. The key word on the environmental side (corresponding with the word 'dependence') is 'reliability' — that is, human, not mechanical, reliability.

The study of the mother's adaptation to infant needs is a fascinating one, and shows that she starts with a high capacity for knowing what the baby needs by being able to identify with the baby. In a graduated way she de-adapts, as one might say, and soon she struggles to get free from this confinement of preoccupation with one baby and the needs of one baby. Without this human environmental provision, the baby does not make the developmental grades that are inherited as tendencies. You can translate this that concerns babies into language that applies to the school ages.

Out of this highly complex field for study there comes a matter which concerns this basic thing: the concept of unity.

For the baby there comes first a unity that includes the

mother. If all goes well, the baby comes to perceive the mother and all other objects and to see these as not-me, so that there is now me and not-me. (Me can take in and contain not-me elements, etc.) This stage of the beginnings of I AM can only come to actuality in the baby's self-establishment in so far as the behaviour of the mother-figure is good enough – i.e. in respect of adaptation and of de-adaptation. So in this respect she is at first a delusion which the baby has to be able to disallow, and there needs to be substituted the uncomfortable I AM unit which involves loss of the merged-in original unit, which is safe. The baby's ego is strong if there is the mother's ego support to make it strong; else it is feeble.

I wonder how disorders in this area affect the learning and teaching of arithmetic? Certainly they could affect the relationship between the pupil and the teacher. Teachers of all kinds do need to know when they are concerned *not with teaching their subject*, but with psychotherapy – that is, completing uncompleted tasks that represent parental failure or relative failure. The task I refer to here is one of giving ego support where it is needed. The opposite is to laugh at a child's failures, especially when these represent fear of forward movement and triumph.

I think it is well known that the relationship between pupil and teacher is always vitally important. This is what psychiatrists usually start off with when referring to teaching problems. Unreliability in the teacher makes almost any child disintegrate. When a child tells us that sums (or history or English) are difficult, the first thing we think of is that the teacher may not be suitable. Sarcasm in a teacher has withered the growing point of many a child's learning. Nevertheless, I do not easily blame the teacher. It is often the child who is insecure or oversensitive, and however careful the teacher may be, the child becomes suspicious. Each case deserves close scrutiny, because no two children are alike, even when each of the two has a difficulty in doing mathematics.

I would like to start now on an examination of the theory

of teaching, in terms of the theory of individual development, but I must leave this aside. I will say, however, that it must be fascinating to see how, in the teaching of mathematics, *one can catch on to the creative impulse*, perhaps the play gesture of a child, and then use this and the child's reaching out, giving all that the child can take by way of teaching until the child comes to the end, for the time being, of the creative reaching out. Sometimes such work can be done better in individual coaching, especially where there is some mending to be done, because the child has had unfortunate experiences, even the experience of bad teaching, which is a form of indoctrination.

Creativity is inherent in playing, and perhaps not to be found elsewhere. A child's play may be to move the head slightly so that in the interplay of the curtain against a line on the wall outside, a line is now one and now two. This can occupy a child (or an adult) for hours. Can you tell me whether a baby fed at two breasts knows of two, or is this at first a reduplication of one? You may be able to catch on to these play activities, but I don't know how. I guess you know the answers to these problems. For me, I feel I must get back to my last, which is quite simply the treatment psychiatrically of ill children, and the construction of a better, more accurate, and more serviceable theory of the emotional development of the individual human being.

Finally, why is it, I ask, that maths is the best example of a subject that can only be taught in continuity? If a stage has been left out, the rest is nonsense. Chickenpox, I think, accounts for many cases of mathematical breakdown (in the Spring term), and if you have time you coach the child over the bit that he or she missed while at home or in quarantine.

This must seem to you to be a muddle. But I am contented simply to take part in an exercise in cross-fertilization. Who knows what hybrid might mongrelize as a result?

The Concept of the False Self

*Unfinished draft of a talk given to 'Crime – A
Challenge', an Oxford University Group, at All
Souls College, Oxford, 29 January 1964*

I have had the honour of addressing 'Crime – A
Challenge' before, and I have found out therefore that your
speakers can choose any subject, not necessarily one that is
related to crime. This leaves me with a difficulty, however,
for if I may speak of absolutely anything, how shall I choose?

Six months ago, when you invited me to be a speaker this
term, I threw up the idea of the concept of a true and false
self, and now I must try to make this into a contribution
which you can feel to be worth discussing.

It is easy to talk about crime, because I know that you are
not criminals. How shall I talk, however, about this, my
chosen subject, without seeming to be preaching a sermon,
since in some form or other or to some degree each one of us
is divided in this way, into a true and a false self? In fact, I
shall need to link the normal with the abnormal and I must
ask your forbearance if in the process I seem to suggest that
all of us are ill or, on the other hand, that the mentally ill are
sane.

I think you will agree that there is nothing new about the
central idea. Poets, philosophers and seers have always concerned themselves with the idea of a true self, and the betrayal
of the self has been a typical example of the unacceptable.
Shakespeare, perhaps to avoid being smug, gathered together
a bundle of truths and handed them out to us by the mouth

of a crashing bore called Polonius. In this way we can take the advice:

> This above all: to thine own self be true,
> And it must follow, as the night the day,
> Thou canst not then be false to any man.

You could quote to me from almost any poet of standing and show that this is a pet theme of people who feel intensely. Also, you could point out to me that present-day drama is searching for the true core within what is square, sentimental, successful or slick.

Let me take it for granted that this same theme haunts the whole of adolescence and even finds echoes in the vast halls of Oxford and Cambridge colleges. There may be some here now who are concerned with the same thing in themselves, as I am myself, but I promise I will not put forward any solutions; if we have these personal problems, we must live with them and see how time brings some kind of personal evolution rather than a solution.

You know that I spend my time treating patients (psychoanalysis and child psychiatry), and as I look round those who are in my care at the present time, I think I see this problem in all of them. Perhaps there is a link between the concept of maturity, or personal adult health, and the solution of this problem of personality. It is as if after years and years on the horns of a dilemma, we suddenly wake up and find the beast was a unicorn.

In one way I am simply saying that each person has a polite or socialized self, and also a personal private self that is not available except in intimacy. This is what is commonly found, and we could call it normal.

If you look around, you can see that *in health* this splitting of the self is an achievement of personal growth; *in illness* the split is a matter of a schism in the mind that can go to any depth; at its deepest it is labelled schizophrenia.

I am therefore talking about common matters that are also matters of utmost significance and seriousness.

While I am in the middle of writing this, I am interrupted by an interview with a child.

He is a boy of ten and the son of a colleague. He has an urgent problem. He is living in a good home, but this does not alter the fact that life is difficult for him, as for others. His particular problem at the present time is that he has become transformed at school after having been consistently difficult and unsuccessful. He has started to learn and to do well. Everyone is delighted and he was referred to as 'a twentieth-century miracle'. There is a complication, however. This change in him has been accompanied by another change which is not so good. He cannot get to sleep. He said to his parents, who are very understanding: 'It's this doing well at school that's the trouble. It's awful. It's girlish.' Lying awake, he has all sorts of worries, which include the idea of his father's death and his own. He thinks a lot about some character in history who worked hard and died at sixteen. This boy was quite specific about the connection between his worries and the change in his character. It was after getting his first 'good' at school; as he got off the bus he suddenly had a new kind of fear, a fear that a man he saw was going to come and kill him. There was a complication to this even, that the idea of being killed was pleasurable to him. He said: 'I can't sleep because if I shut my eyes I get stabbed.'

I am leaving out a very great deal in order to present this case in a way that can be used in this context. In the course of an easy interview that he and I had with each other, he told me of his dreams. One of these is specially significant. He drew a picture of himself in bed with a murderer and a sword, and then there was himself sitting up very frightened with his hand to his mouth, and the murderer just on the point of shoving the sword into him. You can see in this the mixture of murder and symbolic sexual assault, and this would be a not-uncommon dream of a boy of this age. The point is that in talking to me about these matters this boy of ten was able to explain to me that if he does well, then he and his father get on well together, but after a time the boy begins to lose his identity. At this point he becomes defiant and in some silly way refuses to do what he is told. He hates to get into a wrangle with his father, and he usually manages to switch it round to making the masters at school angry with him. In this way he feels real. If he is good, then the dream turns up with the murderer and he is terrified, not so much of being murdered as of getting over into the position of wanting to be murdered, and this makes him feel identified with girls rather than boys.

You see, he really has a problem, a very common one, but perhaps because of the satisfactoriness of the relationship between him and his parents, he is able to express himself clearly. In one language, he can employ a false self which pleases everyone, but this makes him feel awful. In some cases it would make a person feel unreal, but for this boy the trouble is that he feels threatened, as if he were going to be turned into a female or the passive partner in an assault. He is sorely tempted, therefore, to reassert something which is more along the lines of a true self and to be continuously defiant and unsatisfactory, although this too produces no satisfactory answer to his problem.

I am giving this case because I think the boy is rather normal and I think it illustrates the idea that I have put forward already: that the working out of this problem is one of the things that is being done by the adolescent. You will perhaps recognize the same problem in people you know who could be doing well and getting first-class honours degrees and all that sort of thing, but who feel that in some way or other this makes them feel unreal, and that in order to establish a sense of feeling real, they become uncomfortable members of society; you can see them almost deliberately doing badly and disappointing everybody.

This is the awful thing about examinations, all of which are in a sense initiation rites. It starts off with the eleven-plus and goes on through the O- and A-levels to the university degree; and it seems that what is being tested is not only the individual's intellectual capacity, which could be done better by an I Q test, but also the individual's capacity to comply and to tolerate being false, to some degree, in order to gain something in relation to society which can be used while life is being worked out after the phase in which a student's privileges and obligations provide a very special place, which unfortunately does not last for ever.

You can probably feel that there are some people in the world who can quite easily tolerate being compliant in a limited way in order to gain limited advantages, whereas others become thoroughly worked up about this same problem. Naturally, if it comes to this, that someone who is in a muddle over these matters asks for advice, the adviser must come down on the side of the true self, or whatever you like to call it. Whenever there is an insoluble problem over this subject, the outsider must always respect the individual's integrity. Nevertheless, if you are the parent of a boy or girl, you naturally hope that the battle of the true and false selves will not have to be fought out in the territory covered by the words 'teaching' and 'learning'. There is so much to be gained and so much to be enjoyed in this field that it is tragic for a parent to watch when a boy or girl must be antisocial, or, at any rate, the opposite of pro-social, during the time when there is opportunity for the individual to enrich himself or herself culturally.

Perhaps you can understand what I am saying if I take this matter back to early childhood. You teach your small child to say 'thank you'. Actually, you teach your child to say 'thank you' out of politeness and not because this is what the child means. In other words, you start up teaching good manners and you hope that your child will be able to tell lies, that is to say, to be able to conform to convention just to that degree which makes life manageable. You know perfectly well that the child does not always mean 'thank you'. Most children become able to accept this dishonesty as a price to pay for socialization. Some children can never do this. Either someone tried to teach them to say 'ta' too early or else they themselves were tremendously caught up in this problem of integrity. Certainly there are children who would rather be counted out socially than tell a lie.

In describing this I am still talking about normal children. If I go a little further, however, I am talking about children who are going to find life difficult because of this need that they have to establish and to re-establish the importance of the true self relative to anything false. I suppose that it would be true in a general way to say that although a compromise is usually possible in everyday life, there is no compromise for each individual in some area that is chosen for a special treatment. It may be science or religion or poetry or games. In the chosen area there is no room for compromise.

The Value of Depression

A paper given to a General Meeting of the Association of Psychiatric Social Workers, September 1963

The term 'depression' has a popular and a professional psychiatric meaning. Curiously enough, these two meanings are very much like each other. Perhaps, if this is true, there is a reason that can be stated. The affective state or disorder, depression, carries with it hypochondria and introspection; the depressed person is therefore aware of feeling awful and also aware to an exaggerated degree of heart, lungs and liver, and of rheumatic pains. By contrast, the psychiatric term 'hypomania', perhaps equivalent to the psychoanalytic term 'manic-defence', implies that a depressed mood is being negated, and seems to have no popular equivalent. (The Greek hubris might do. But hubris and hubristic seem to imply elation rather than hypomania.)

The view is expressed here that depression has value; yet it is also clear that depressed people suffer, that they may hurt themselves or end their lives, that some of them are psychiatric casualties. There is a paradox here which I wish to examine.

Psychoanalysts and psychiatric social workers find themselves taking responsibility for serious cases and becoming involved in giving psychotherapy when, at the same time, they are not themselves by any means free from depression. And since constructive work is one of the best things to come out of depression, it often happens that we use our work with depressives (and others) to deal with our own depressions.

As a medical student I was taught that *depression has within itself the germ of recovery*. This is the one bright spot in psychopathology, and it links depression with the sense of guilt (a capacity for which is a sign of healthy development) and with the mourning process. Mourning too tends eventually to finish its job. The built-in tendency to recover links depression also with the maturation process of the individual's infancy and childhood, a process which (in a facilitating environment) leads on to personal maturity, which is health.

Individual Emotional Development

In the beginning the infant is the environment and the environment is the infant. By a complex process (which is in part understood, and on which I and others have written at great length)[1] the infant separates out objects and then the *environment* from the *self*. There is a half-way state in which the object to which the infant is related is a subjective object.

Then the infant becomes a *unit*, first momentarily and then almost all the time. One of many consequences of this new development is that the infant comes to have an *inside*. A complex interchange between what is inside and what is outside now begins, and continues throughout the individual's life, and constitutes the main relationship of the individual to the world. This relationship is more important

1. D. W. Winnicott, 'Paediatrics and Psychiatry' and 'Transitional Objects and Transitional Phenomena', in *Collected Papers: Through Paediatrics to Psycho-Analysis*, London, Tavistock Publications, 1958.

M. Balint, 'Three Areas of the Mind', *International Journal of Psycho-Analysis*, vol. 39, 1958.

M. Milner, 'Aspects of the Symbolism of the Comprehension of the Not-Self', *International Journal of Psycho-Analysis*, vol. 33, 1952.

W. Hoffer, 'The Mutual Influences in the Development of Ego and Id: Earliest Stages', in *The Psychoanalytic Study of the Child*, Volume 7, 1952.

even than object-relating and instinct gratification. This two-way interchange involves mental mechanisms that are named 'projection' and 'introjection'. And then much happens, in fact, very much indeed, but it would be out of place to develop this statement further in this context.

The source of these developments is the inborn *maturational process* in the individual, which the environment facilitates. The facilitating environment is necessary, and without its being *good enough*, the maturational process weakens or wilts. (I have often described these matters, and they are complex.)[2]

Thus, *ego structure* and *strength* become a fact, and the dependence of a new individual on the environment moves further and further away from the absolute and towards independence, though never reaching to absolute independence.

The development and establishment of ego strength is the important or basic feature indicating health. Naturally the term 'ego strength' comes to mean more and more as the child matures, and at first the ego has strength only because of the ego support given by the adapting mother, who for a while is able to identify closely with her own infant.

There comes a stage at which the child has become a unit, becomes able to feel: I AM, has an inside, is able to ride his or her instinctual storms, and also is able to *contain the strains and stresses* that arise in the personal inner psychic reality. *The child has become able to be depressed*. This is an achievement of emotional growth.

Our view of depression, then, is closely bound up with our concept of ego strength and of self-establishment and of the discovery of a personal identity, and it is for this reason that we can discuss the idea that depression has value.

2. D. W. Winnicott, 'The Observation of Infants in a Set Situation' and 'Clinical Varieties of Transference', in *Collected Papers: Through Paediatrics to Psycho-Analysis*, London, Tavistock Publications, 1958.

D. W. Winnicott, 'Psycho-Analysis and the Sense of Guilt', in *The Maturational Processes and the Facilitating Environment*, London, Hogarth Press, 1965.

In clinical psychiatry, depression may have features that make it obviously a description of illness, but always, even in severe affective disorders, the presence of the depressed mood gives some ground for belief that the individual ego is not disrupted and may be able to hold the fort, if not actually come through to some sort of resolution of the internal war.

Psychology of Depression

Not everyone admits that there is a psychology of depression at all. For many people (including some psychiatrists) it is almost a religious belief that depression is biochemical, or a modern equivalent of the black bile theory which enabled a medieval genius to coin the name 'melancholia'. You must expect to meet a powerful resistance to the idea of there being an unconscious positive mental organization giving a psychological meaning to mood. But for me there is a meaning to mood and to its various impurities leading to pathological features, and I shall try to describe some of what I know. (What I know is based on what I have found in my work, in which I apply theories that are my own and that are derived from Freud, Klein and several other pioneers.)

Naturally, hate is locked up somewhere in all this. Perhaps the difficulty is in accepting such hate, even though the depressed mood implies that hate is under control. It is the clinical effort at control that we are seeing.

Simple Case of Depression Allied to Psychoneurosis

A girl of fourteen was brought to Paddington Green Children's Hospital because of depression heavy enough to make her school work deteriorate seriously. In one psychotherapeutic interview (one hour) the girl described and drew a nightmare in which her mother was run over by a car. The driver of the car had a cap like her father's. I interpreted to her her powerful love for her father in order to explain her having the idea of her mother's death, whilst at the same time it was sexual intercourse that was represented in violent terms. She saw that the reason for the nightmare was sexual tension and love. She now accepted the fact of her hate of her mother, to whom she was devoted. Her mood lifted. She went home free from depression, and became able to enjoy school work again. The improvement lasted.

This is the simplest type of case. When a dream is dreamed, remembered, and appropriately reported, this in itself is an indication that the dreamer has the capacity to cope with the inner tensions that belong to the dream. The dream that was also drawn indicated ego strength, and, moreover, the content of the dream gave a sample of the dynamics of the girl's personal inner psychic reality.

Here one could speak of repressed hate and the death wish in the heterosexual position, leading to inhibition of the instinctual impulses. What is characteristic, however, would be omitted in this language, that is to say, the mood, the girl's personal unaliveness. If she became alive, her mother became hurt. This is a sense of guilt operating in advance.

The Self as a Unit

If you accept diagrams, it is helpful to think of the person as represented by a sphere or circle. Inside the circle is collected all the interplay of forces and objects that constitute the inner reality of the individual at this moment in time. The details of this inner world are rather like a map of Berlin with the Berlin Wall symbolizing a locus for the world's tensions.

In this diagram, a fog over the city – if they have fogs there – represents the depressed mood. Everything is slowed down and brought towards a state of deadness. This state of relative deadness controls all, and in the case of the human individual blurs instincts and the capacity for relating to external objects. Gradually the fog gets thin in places or even begins to lift. And then there may be surprising phenomena that help, like the chink in the Wall at Christmas time. The mood lessens in intensity and life begins again, here and there, where tensions are less. So rearrangements take place, an East German escapes to West Germany and perhaps a West German transfers over to the East. Somehow or other exchanges occur, and so the time comes when it is safe for the mood to pass. In the human example the equivalent of the Wall will have shifted a little from East to West or from West to East, which cannot happen in Berlin.

The mood and its resolution is a matter of the arrangement of good and bad internal elements, a structuralization of a war. It is like the dining-room table where a boy has arranged his fort and soldiers.

Girls tend to keep the elements subjective – not specific – because they can think of possible pregnancies and infants. Infants naturally counter the idea of lifelessness within. The girls' potential is envied by the boys.

Here consideration is being given not so much to anxiety and to anxiety content, as to ego structure and the internal economy of the individual. Depression coming on, continuing and lifting, indicates that the ego structure has held over a phase of crisis. This is a triumph of integration.

Nature of Crisis

We can only glance at the way crises arise, and also at certain types of relief.

The prime cause of the depressed mood is a new experience of destructiveness and of destructive ideas that go with loving. The new experiences necessitate internal reassessment, and it is this reassessment we see as depression.

And about things that offer relief – these are not reassurances. It is no good offering cheer to a depressed person or jogging the depressed child up and down, offering sweetmeats and pointing to the trees and saying: 'See the lovely shimmering green leaves.' To the depressed person the tree looks dead and the leaves are still. Or there are no leaves and there is only the black and blasted heath and the barren landscape. We only make fools of ourselves if we offer good cheer.

What may make a difference is a really good persecution: threat of war, for instance, or a spiteful nurse in the mental hospital, or a piece of treachery. Here the external bad phenomenon can be used as a place for some of the internal badness, and produce relief by projection of inner tensions; the fog may start to lift. But one can hardly prescribe evil. (Perhaps shock treatment is evil deliberately prescribed, and therefore sometimes successful clinically, though a form of cheating if one thinks in terms of the human dilemma.)

But one can help a depressed person by adopting the principle of tolerating the depression until it spontaneously lifts, and by paying tribute to the fact that it is only the spontaneous recovery that feels truly satisfactory to the individual. Certain conditions affect the outcome, or hasten it or retard it. The most important is the state of the individual's inner economy. Is it in any case precarious? Or is there in it a reserve of benign elements in the forces ranged against each other in the perpetual armed neutrality of the inner economy?

To our surprise, a person may come out of a depression stronger, wiser and more stable than before he or she went into it. A great deal depends, however, on the freedom of the depression from what might be called 'impurities'. An attempt will be made to indicate what may be the nature of such impurities.

Impurities of Depression Mood

1. In this category I will place all *the failures of ego organization* which indicate a tendency in the patient towards a more primitive type of illness, towards schizophrenia. Here the threat of disintegration exists and it is psychotic defences (splitting, etc.) that give the clinical picture, which includes splitting, depersonalization, unreality feelings and lack of touch with internal reality. There may be a diffuse schizoid

element complicating depression so that the term 'schizoid depression' can be used. This term implies that some general ego organization (depression) is maintained in spite of the disintegration that threatens (schizoid).

2. In this second category I will place those patients who maintain the ego structure that makes depression possible and yet who have *delusions of persecution*. The presence of such delusions indicates that the patient is either using adverse external factors or the memory of traumata to obtain relief from the full blast of the internal persecutions, the blanketing of which results in a depressed mood.

3. In this third category I refer to the relief that patients get from the inner tensions in allowing these to become expressed in *hypochondriacal terms*. The presence of somatic illness can be used, or as in the case of delusions of persecution (Category 2), somatic illness may be imagined, or produced by distortions of the physiological processes.

4. In this category I refer to a different type of impurity, one which is expressed in the psychiatric term *hypomania* and is referred to in the psychoanalytic term *manic-defence*. Here depression exists, but is denied or negated. Each detail of depression (deadness, heaviness, darkness, seriousness, etc.) is supplanted by its opposite (aliveness, lightness, luminosity, flippancy, etc.); this is a useful defence, but the individual pays for it by the return of the inevitable depression to be endured privately.

5. In this category I refer to the *manic-depressive swing*. This somewhat resembles the changes from depression to manic-defence, but is really very different because of a certain feature, a dissociation relative to the two states. In the manic-depressive swing the patient is either depressed because of controlling an inner tension or else is maniacal (not manic) because of being possessed and activated by some aspect of the tense inner situation. *In either swing of mood the patient is not in touch with the condition that belongs to the other swing.*

6. Here I will refer to the *exaggeration of ego boundaries* which belongs to the fear of a breakdown into schizoid splitting mechanisms. The result, clinically, is a fierce organization of the personality in a depressive pattern. This may persist unaltered over a long period of time and become built in to the patient's personality.

7. In *sulking and melancholia* there is a kind of 'return of the repressed'. Although all hate and destruction is controlled, the clinical state effected by this controlling is in itself unbearable to those in contact with the patient. The *mood* is antisocial and destructive, although the patient's hate is unavailable and fixed.

It is not possible to develop these themes further here and now. What is to be emphasized is the ego strength and personal maturity that is manifested in the 'purity' of the depression mood.

Summary

Depression belongs to psychopathology. It can be severe and crippling and may last a lifetime, and it is commonly a passing mood in relatively healthy individuals. At the normal end, depression, which is a common, almost universal, phenomenon, relates to mourning, to the capacity to feel guilt, and to the maturational process. Always, depression implies ego strength, and in this way depression tends to lift, and the depressed person tends to recover in mental health.

Aggression, Guilt
and Reparation

*A talk given to the Progressive League, 8 May
1960*

I wish to draw on my experience as a psychoanalyst
to describe a theme which comes up over and over again in
analytic work and which is always of great importance. It has
to do with one of the roots of constructive activity. It has to
do with the relationship between construction and destruction. You may immediately recognize this theme as one which
has been developed chiefly by Melanie Klein, who has
gathered together her ideas on the subject under the heading,
'The Depressive Position in Emotional Development'.
Whether this is a good name or not is beside the point. The
main thing is that psychoanalytic theory evolves all the time,
and it was Mrs Klein who took up the destructiveness that is
in human nature and started to make sense of it in psychoanalytic terms. This was an important development that came
in the decade after the First World War and many of us
feel that our work could not have been done without this
important addition to Freud's own statement of the emotional
development of the human being. Melanie Klein's work
extended Freud's own statement, and did not alter the analyst's way of working.

It might be thought that this subject belongs to the
teaching of the psychoanalytic technique. If I judge the situation correctly, you would not mind even this. I do believe,
however, that the subject is of vital importance to all thinking
people, especially as it enriches our understanding of the

meaning of the term 'a sense of guilt', by joining up the sense of guilt on the one hand to destructiveness and on the other hand to constructive activity.

It all sounds rather simple and obvious. Ideas of destroying an object turn up, a sense of guilt appears, and constructive work results. But what is found is very much more complex and it is important when attempting a comprehensive description to remember that it is an achievement in the emotional development of an individual when this simple sequence begins to make sense or to be a fact or to be significant.

It is characteristic of psychoanalysts that when they try to tackle a subject like this, they always think in terms of the *developing individual*. This means going back very early and looking to see if the point of origin can be determined. Certainly it would be possible to think of earliest infancy as a state in which the individual has not a capacity for feeling guilty. Then one can say that at a later date we know that (in health) a sense of guilt can be felt, or experienced without perhaps being registered as such in consciousness. In between these two things is a period in which the capacity for a sense of guilt is in the process of becoming established, and it is with this period that I am concerned in this paper.

It is not necessary to give ages and dates, but I would say that parents can sometimes detect the beginnings of a sense of guilt before their infant is a year old, though no one would think that before the age of five there has become firmly established in a child a technique for accepting full responsibility for destructive ideas. In dealing with this development we know we are talking about the whole of childhood, particularly about adolescence; and if we are talking about adolescence, we are talking about adults, because no adults are all the time adult. This is because people are not just their own age; they are to some extent every age, or no age.

In passing, I would like to say that it seems to me that it is comparatively easy for us to get at the destructiveness that is in ourselves when this is linked with anger at frustration or hate of something we disapprove of or when it is a reaction to fear. The difficult thing is for each individual to take full responsibility for the destructiveness that is personal, and that inherently belongs to a relationship to an object that is felt to be good – in other words, that is related to loving.

'Integration' is a word that comes in here, because if one can conceive of a fully integrated person, then that person takes full responsibility for *all* feelings and ideas that belong to being alive. By contrast, it is a failure of integration when we need to find the things we disapprove of outside ourselves and do so at a price – this price being the loss of the de-structiveness which really belongs to ourselves.

I am talking, therefore, about the development which has to take place in every individual of the capacity to take re-sponsibility for the whole of that individual's feelings and ideas, the word 'health' being closely linked with the degree of integration which makes it possible for this to happen. One thing about a healthy person is that he or she does not have to use in a big way the technique of projection in order to cope with his or her own destructive impulses and thoughts.

You will understand that I am passing over the earliest stages, the things that one can call the primitive aspects of emotional development. Shall I say I am not talking about the first weeks or months? A breakdown in this area of basic emotional development leads to mental hospital illness, that is to say, schizophrenia, with which I am not dealing in this lecture. In this paper I assume that in each case the parents have made the essential provision which has enabled the infant to start leading an individual existence. What I want to say could apply equally to the care of a normal child during a certain stage of development or to a phase in the treatment of a child or an adult, for in psychotherapy nothing really new ever happens; the best that can happen is that something that was not completed in an individual's development originally becomes to some extent completed at a later date, in the course of the treatment.

My intention now is to give you some examples from analytic treatments. I shall leave out everything except the details that are relevant to the idea I am trying to put forward.

Case 1

One example comes from the analysis of someone who is himself doing psychotherapy. He started off a session by telling me that he had been to see one of his own patients performing, that is to say, he had gone outside the role of therapist dealing with the patient in the consulting room and had seen this patient at work. This work involved very quick movements and was highly skilled, and the patient was very successful in this peculiar job in which he uses quick movements which in the therapeutic hour make no sense, but which move him round on the couch as if he were possessed. My patient (who is the therapist of this man) was doubtful about what he had done, whether it was good or not, although he felt that probably it was a good thing for him to see this man at work. He then made a reference to his own activities in the Easter holidays. He has a country house and he very much enjoys physical labour and all kinds of constructive activity, and he likes gadgets, which he really uses. He then went on to describe events in his home life. I need not pass these on with all their emotional colouring, but I will simply say that he returned to a theme which has been important in the recent analysis in which various kinds of engineering tools have played a large part. On his way to the analytic session he often stops and gazes at a machine tool in a shop window near my house. This has the most splendid teeth. This is my patient's way of getting at his oral aggression, the primitive love impulse with all its ruthlessness and destructiveness. We could call it eating. The trend in his treatment is towards this ruthlessness of primitive loving, and, as can be imagined, the resistance against getting to it is tremendous. (Incidentally, this man knows the theory, and could give a good account of all these processes in an intellectual way, but he comes for postgraduate analysis because he needs to get truly in touch with his primitive impulses as a matter not of the mind, but of instinctual experience and of bodily feeling.) There was much else in the hour's content, including a discussion of the question: can one eat one's cake and have it?

The only thing I want to pull out of this is the observation that when this new material came up relating to primitive love and to the destruction of the object, *there had already been* some reference to constructive work. When I made the interpretation that the patient needed from me, about his destruction of me (eating), I could remind him of what he had said about construction. I could remind him that just as he saw his patient performing, and the performance made sense of the jerky movements, so I might have seen him working in his garden, using gadgets in order to improve the property. He could cut through walls and trees, and it was all enjoyed tremendously, but if this had come apart from the constructive aim, it would have been a senseless, maniacal episode. This is a regular feature in our work, and it is the theme of my talk this evening.

Perhaps it is true to say that human beings cannot tolerate the destructive aim in their very early loving. The idea of it can be tolerated, however, if the individual who is getting towards it has evidence of a constructive aim already at hand of which he or she can be reminded.

I am thinking here of the treatment of a woman. Early on in the treatment I made a mistake which nearly ended everything. I interpreted this very thing, oral sadism, the ruthless eating of the object belonging to primitive loving. I had plenty of evidence, and indeed I was right, but the interpretation was given ten years too soon. I learned my lesson. In the long treatment that followed, the patient reorganized herself and became a real and integrated person who could accept the truth about her primitive impulses. Eventually she became ready for this interpretation after ten or twelve years of daily analysis.

Case 2

A man patient came into my room and saw a tape recorder that had been lent me. This gave him ideas, and he said, as he lay down and gathered himself together for the work of the analytic hour: 'I would like to think that when I have finished treatment what has happened here with me will be of value to the world in some way or other.' I made a mental note that this remark *might* indicate that the patient was near to one of those bouts of destructiveness with which I had had to deal repeatedly since the treatment started two years ago. Before the end of the hour the patient had truly reached a new acquaintance with his envy of me for my being some good as an analyst. He had the impulse to thank me for being good, and for being able to do what he needed me to do. We had had all this before, but he was now, more than he had been on previous occasions, in touch with his destructive feelings towards what might be called a good object. When all this had been thoroughly established, I reminded him of his hope, expressed as he came in and saw the tape recorder, that his treatment might of itself prove valuable, something that would contribute in to the general pool of human need. (It was not, of course, *necessary* for me to remind him of this, because the important thing was what had happened, not the discussion of what had happened.)

When I linked these two things, he said that this felt right, but how awful it would have been if I had interpreted on the basis of this first remark; he meant, if I had taken up his wish to be of use and told him that this indicated a wish to destroy. He had to reach to the destructive urge first, and he had to reach it in his own time and in his own way. No doubt it was his capacity to have an idea of ultimately contributing that was making it possible for him to get into more intimate contact with his destructiveness. But constructive effort is false and worse than meaningless unless, as he said, he has first reached to the destruction. He felt that his work hitherto had been without proper foundation, and indeed (as he reminded me) it was for this that he came to me for treatment. Incidentally, he has done very good work, but always as he gets towards success he feels an increasing sense of futility

and falseness, and a need to prove his worthlessness. This
has been his life pattern.

Case 3

A woman colleague is talking about a man patient. This
man reaches to material which can properly be interpreted
as an impulse to steal from the analyst. He in fact says to
her, after experiencing a good piece of analytic work, 'I
now find I hate you for your insight, the very thing I need
of you; I have the impulse to steal from you whatever
there is in you that makes you able to do this work.' Now,
just before this, he had said (in passing) how nice it would
be to earn more money so as to be able to pay a higher fee.
You will see the same thing here: a platform of generosity
reached and used so that from it a glimpse might be gained
of the envy, the stealing and the destructiveness of the
good object, that which underlies the generosity, and
which belongs to primitive loving.

Case 4

The next snippet comes out of a long case description of
an adolescent girl who is having treatment from someone
who is at the same time looking after the child in her own
home, along with her own children. This arrangement has
advantages and disadvantages.

The girl has been severely ill, and at the time of the
incident I shall recount she was emerging from a long
period of regression to dependence and to an infantile state.
It could be said that now the girl was not regressed in her
relation to the home and the family, but is still in a very
special state in the limited area of the treatment sessions.
These occur at a set time in the evenings.

A time came when this girl expressed the very deepest
hate of Mrs X (who is both caring for her and doing her
treatment). All was well in the rest of the twenty-four
hours, but in the treatment area Mrs X was destroyed
utterly and repeatedly. It is difficult to convey the degree
of her hate of Mrs X, the therapist, and, in fact, her annihilation of her. Here it was not a case of the therapist

going out to see the patient at work, for Mrs X had the girl in her care all the time and there were two separate relationships going on between them simultaneously. In the day all sorts of new things began to happen: the girl began to want to help to clean the house, to polish the furniture, to be of use. This helping was absolutely new and had never been a feature in this girl's personal pattern in her own home, even before she became acutely ill.

I should think that there must be few adolescents who have, in fact, done so little at home to help; she had not even helped with the washing-up. So this helping was quite a new feature and it happened silently (so to speak) alongside the utter destructiveness that the child began to find in the primitive aspects of her loving which she reached in her relation to the therapist in the therapy sessions.

You see the same idea repeating itself here. Naturally, the fact that the patient was becoming conscious of the destructiveness made possible the constructive activity which appeared in the day. But it is the other way round that I want you to see this just now. The constructive and creative experiences were making it possible for the child to get to the experience of her destructiveness.

You will observe a corollary, which is that the patient needs opportunity for contributing in, and this is where my subject links up with ordinary living. Opportunity for creative activity, for imaginative playing, and for constructive working – this is just what we try to give equally for everyone. I shall refer to this again.

I now want to try to put together the ideas that I have put forward in the form of case material.

We are dealing with one aspect of the sense of guilt. It comes from toleration of one's destructive impulses in primitive loving. Toleration of one's destructive impulses results in a new thing: the capacity to enjoy ideas, even with destruction in them, and the bodily excitements that belong to them, or that they belong to. This development gives elbow-room for the experience of concern, which is the basis for everything constructive.

You will see that various pairs of words can be used according to the stage of emotional development that is being described:

> Annihilation . . . creating
> Destruction . . . re-creating
> Hating . . . reinforced loving
> Being cruel . . . being tender
> Soiling . . . cleaning
> Damaging . . . mending

and so on.

Let me put my thesis this way. If you like, you can look at the way a person mends, and you can cleverly say: 'Aha, that means unconscious destruction.' But the world is not helped on much if you do this. Alternatively, you may see in someone's mending that he or she is building up a self-strength which makes possible a toleration of the destructiveness that belongs to that person's nature. Say you somehow block the mending: then to some extent that person becomes unable to take responsibility for his or her destructive urges, and clinically the result is either depression or else a search for relief by the discovery of destructiveness elsewhere – that is to say, by the mechanism of projection.

To end this brief exposition of a vast subject, let me list some of the everyday applications of the work that underlies what I have said:

1. Opportunity for contributing in, in some way or other, helps each one of us to accept the destructiveness that is part of ourselves, basic, and belonging to loving, which is eating.

2. Providing opportunity, being perceptive when people have constructive moments, does not necessarily work, and we can see why this should be so.

3. We give opportunity for contributing in to someone, and we may get three results:

(*a*) That is just what was needed.

(*b*) The opportunity is falsely used, and eventually the

constructive activities become withdrawn because they are felt to be false.

(*c*) Opportunity offered to someone who is unable to get to the personal destructiveness is felt as a reproach and the result is disastrous clinically.

4. We may use the ideas I have discussed in order to enjoy some intellectual understanding of the way a sense of guilt works, being at the point of transformation of destructiveness into constructiveness. (It must be pointed out here that ordinarily the sense of guilt I am talking about is silent, not conscious. It is a potential sense of guilt, annulled by the constructive activities. Clinical sense of guilt that is a conscious burden is rather another matter.)

5. From this we reach some understanding of the compulsive destructiveness which may appear anywhere, but which is a special problem of adolescence and a regular feature of the antisocial tendency. Destructiveness, though compulsive and spoof, is more honest than constructiveness when the latter is not properly founded on the sense of guilt that arises out of acceptance of one's personal destructive urges directed towards the object that is felt to be good.

6. These matters relate to the tremendously important things that are going on in rather an obscure fashion when a mother and a father are giving their new baby a good start in life.

7. Finally, we arrive at the fascinating and philosophic question: can one eat one's cake and have it?

Delinquency as a Sign of Hope

*A talk given to the Borstal Assistant Governors'
Conference, held at King Alfred's College,
Winchester, April 1967*

Although the title of my talk has been put in the
programme in the following form: 'Delinquency as a Sign of
Hope', I would prefer to talk about the 'antisocial tendency'.
The reason is that this term can be applied to tendencies that
appear at the normal end of the scale from time to time in
your own children or in children living in good homes of
their own, and it is here that one can best see the connection
that I believe exists between the tendency and hope. By the
time the boy or girl has become hardened because of the
failure of the communication, the antisocial act not being
recognized as something that contains an SOS, and when
secondary gains have become important, and great skill has
been achieved in some antisocial activity, then it is much
more difficult to see (what is still there, nevertheless) the
SOS that is a signal of hope in the boy or girl who is antisocial.

The second thing that I want to make clear is that I know I
could not do your job. By temperament I am not fitted for
the work that you do; and in any case I am not tall enough or
big enough. I have certain skills and a certain kind of experience, and it remains to be seen whether there can be
some pathway found between the things that I know something about and the work that you are doing. It might happen
that nothing that I say will have any effect at all on what you

do when you go back to your work. Nevertheless, there might be some effect of an *indirect* kind, because it must sometimes seem to you to be an insult to human nature that most of the boys and girls you have to deal with have this tendency to be a nuisance. You try to relate the delinquency you see in front of you to general matters like poverty, poor housing, broken homes, parental delinquency, and a breakdown of the social provision. I would like to feel that as a result of what I have to say, you may be able to see a little more clearly that *in every case that comes your way there was a beginning* and at the beginning there was an illness, and the boy or girl *became a deprived child*. In other words, there is sense in what once happened, although by the time that each individual comes into your care the sense has usually become lost.

A third thing that I want to make clear has to do with the fact that I am a psychoanalyst. I am not putting forward a strong claim that psychoanalysis has a direct contribution to make to your subject. If it has, this belongs to recent work, and I have taken some part personally in trying to formulate a theory, which is valuable because true and which derives to some extent from the general body of understanding that has come through psychoanalysis.

I now come to the main statement that I want to make, which is really not at all complex. According to my view, which is based on experience (but, as I freely admit, on experience of younger children who are near the beginning of their trouble and who are not from the worst social conditions), *the antisocial tendency is linked inherently with deprivation*. In other words, it is not the general social failure that is responsible so much as a specific failure. For the child that we are studying, it can be said that *things went well enough and then they did not go well enough*. A change occurred which altered the whole life of the child and this change in the environment happened when the child was old enough to know about things. It is not that the child could come here and give a lecture on himself or herself but, given suitable conditions, the child is able to reproduce what happened because of having been far enough developed at the time to have been aware. In other words, in special conditions of psychotherapy the child is able to remember in terms of the material produced, in playing or in dreaming or in talking, the essential features of the original deprivation. I want to contrast this with environmental disturbances at an earlier stage of emotional development. A baby deprived of oxygen does not go around hoping to convince someone that if there had been enough oxygen, things would have been all right. Environmental disturbances distorting the emotional development of a baby do not produce the antisocial tendency; they produce distortions of the personality which result in illness of psychotic type, so that the boy or girl is liable to mental hospital disorder or else he or she goes through life with certain distortions of reality testing and so on, perhaps of the kind that are accepted. The antisocial tendency relates not to privation, but to a deprivation.

The characteristic of the antisocial tendency is the drive that it gives the boy or girl to get back behind the deprivation moment or condition. A child who has been deprived in this way has first suffered unthinkable anxiety and then has gradually reorganized into someone who is in a fairly neutral state, complying because there is nothing else that the child is strong enough to do. This state may be fairly satisfactory from the point of view of those who are in charge. Then, for some reason or other, hope begins to appear, and this means that the child, without being conscious of what is going on, begins to have the urge to get back behind the moment of deprivation and so to undo the fear of the *unthinkable anxiety or confusion that resulted before the neutral state became organized*. This is the very deceptive thing that those in care of antisocial children need to know if they are to see sense in what is going on around them. Whenever conditions give a child a certain degree of new hope, *then the antisocial tendency becomes a clinical feature and the child becomes difficult*.

At this point it is necessary to see that we are talking about two aspects of this one thing, the antisocial tendency. I would like to relate one of these to the relationship between the small child and the mother and the other to the later development which is the child's relation to the father. The first one has to do with all children and the second one is more especially the concern of boys. The first one has to do with the fact that the mother in her adaptation to the small child's needs enables the child creatively to find objects. She initiates the creative use of the world. When this fails, the child has lost contact with objects, has lost the capacity creatively to find anything. At the moment of hope the child reaches out and steals an object. This is a compulsive act and the child does not know why he or she does it. Often the child feels mad because of having a compulsion to do something without knowing why. Naturally, the fountain pen stolen from Woolworths is not satisfactory: it is not the object that was being sought, and in any case the child is looking for the capacity to find, not for an object. Nevertheless, there may be some satisfaction belonging to what is done in a moment of hope. The apple stolen from the orchard is more on the borderline. It can be ripe and can taste nice and it can be fun to be chased by the farmer. On the other hand, the apple may be green and, if eaten, may give the boy a stomach-ache, and it may be that already the boy is not eating what he has stolen but is giving the apples away, or perhaps he organizes the theft without running the risk of climbing the wall himself. In this sequence we see the transition from the normal prank to the antisocial act.

And so, if we examine this first kind of expression of the antisocial tendency, we can arrive at something so common as to be normal. Your own child claims the right to go into the larder and take a bun, or your little child of two years explores your wife's handbag and takes out a penny. If we examine all degrees, we find at one extreme something which is hardening into a compulsive act without meaning and without producing direct satisfaction but blossoming into a skill; while at the other extreme is something which happens over and over again in every family: a child reacting to some kind of relative deprivation by an antisocial act and the parents responding by a temporary period of indulgence which may very well see the child through a difficult phase.

Alongside this I want to examine deprivation in terms of the child and the father, but the principle is the same. The child – and this time I will say the boy, because if it is a girl I am still talking about the boy in the girl – finds that it is safe to have aggressive feelings and to be aggressive, because of the framework of the family representing society in a localized form. The mother's confidence in her husband or in the support that she will get, if she calls out, from local society, perhaps from the policeman, makes it possible for the child to explore crudely destructive activities which relate to movement in general, and also more specifically destruction that has to do with the fantasy that accumulates round the hate. In this way (because of the environmental security, mother supported by father, etc.) the child becomes able to do a very complex thing, that is to say, to integrate all his destructive impulses in with the loving ones, and the result when things go well is that the child recognizes the reality of the destructive *ideas* that are inherent in life and living and loving, and finds ways and means of protecting valued people and objects from himself. In fact, he organizes his life constructively in order not to feel too bad about the very real destructiveness that goes on in his mind. In order to achieve this in his development, the child *absolutely requires an environment that is indestructible in essential respects*: certainly carpets get dirtied and the walls have to be re-papered and an occasional window gets broken, but somehow the home sticks together, and behind all this is the confidence that the child has in the relationship between the parents; the family is a going concern. When a deprivation occurs in terms of a breakup of the home, especially an estrangement between the parents, a very severe thing happens in the child's mental organization. Suddenly his aggressive ideas and impulses become unsafe. I think that what happens immediately is that the child takes over the control that has been lost and becomes identified with the framework, the result being that he loses his own impulsiveness and spontaneity. There is much too much anxiety now for experimentation which could result in his coming to terms with his own aggression. There follows a period which again (as in the first type of deprivation) can be fairly satisfactory from the point of view of those in charge, in which the boy is more identified with those in charge than with his own immature self.

The antisocial tendency in this kind of case leads the boy, whenever he feels some sort of hope of a return of security, to rediscover himself, and this means a *rediscovery of his own aggressiveness*. He does not know, of course, what is going on, but he simply finds that he has hurt someone or has broken a window. In this case, therefore, instead of hope leading to an S O S signal in terms of stealing, it leads to an S O S signal in terms of *an outburst of aggression*. The aggression is liable to be senseless and quite divorced from logic, and it is no good asking the child who is aggressive in this way why he has broken the window any more than it is useful to ask a child who has stolen why he took money.

These two clinical types of manifestation of the antisocial tendency are really related to each other. It is simply that, on the whole, the stealing relates to a deprivation that is earlier in terms of the child's emotional growth than is the aggressive outburst. There is something common in society's reaction to both types of antisocial behaviour at this moment of hope. When the child steals or is aggressive, society is liable not only to fail to get the message, but (more than likely) it will feel stimulated to respond moralistically. The natural mass reaction is in the direction of the punishment for stealing and for the maniacal outburst, and every effort is made to force the young criminal to give an explanation in logical terms which, in fact, does not apply. At the end of a few hours of persistent questioning, fingerprint evidence, etc., antisocial children will come up with some kind of confession and explanation simply to bring to an end an interminable and intolerable inquiry. This confession has no value, however, because even though it may contain true facts, it nevertheless cannot get to the true cause or to the *aetiology* of the disturbance. In fact, time which is spent in extortion of confessions and on fact-finding commissions is wasted time.

Although what has been stated here, if correct, may have no bearing on the day-to-day management of a group of boys or girls, it is necessary to examine the situation to see whether under certain circumstances there might possibly be a practical application of theory. Would it be possible, for instance, for someone who is in charge of a group of delinquent boys to arrange for personal contact of a therapeutic kind? In a sense all communities are therapeutic in so far as they work. Children have nothing to gain from living in a chaotic group, and sooner or later, if there is no strong management, a dictator arises among the children. Nevertheless, there is another meaning to the word 'therapeutic' and this has to do with putting oneself in a position in which one can be communicated with from a deep level.

I think that it may be impossible in most cases for those who are in charge day and night to make the necessary adjustment in themselves which would enable them to allow a boy a period of psychotherapy or personal contact. I would certainly not lightly advise anyone to attempt to use the two methods. At the same time, however, I would think that these matters can be managed by some and that the boys (or girls) can make very good use of such specialized therapeutic sessions. What must be emphasized, however, is *the absolute difference that there is in your attitude when you are responsible for general management and when you are in a personal relationship with a child*. To start with, the attitude towards the antisocial manifestation is quite different in the two cases. For someone who is in charge of a group, the antisocial activity is just not acceptable. In the therapeutic session, by contrast, there is no question of morality except that which may turn up in the child. The therapeutic session is not a fact-finding commission and whoever is doing this therapeutic work is not concerned with objective truth, but is very definitely concerned with what feels real to the patient.

There is something here that can be carried right over from psychoanalysis, since psychoanalysts know very well that in some of the sessions with their patients they are accused, for instance, of something of which they are innocent. Patients may accuse them of deliberately changing the place of an object in the room in order to trick them; or they may feel quite certain that the analyst has another patient as a favourite, etc. I am referring to what is called the 'delusional transference'. It would be very natural for an analyst who does not know to defend himself to say, for instance, that the object is in the same place as it was yesterday; or that a simple mistake has been made; or that he does his very best not to favour one person more than another. In doing so the analyst would *fail to use the material that the patient presents*. The patient is experiencing in the present something which has reality at some point in his past, and if the analyst will allow himself to be put in the role allotted, there will be an outcome in the sense that the patient will recover from the delusion. Because of the therapist's need to accept the role allotted at the moment by the patient, it must be very difficult to switch over from the role of group management to one of individual acceptance, but if this can be done, there can be rich rewards. Anyone who wishes to try this must be reminded, however, that this work cannot be lightly undertaken. If a boy is to be seen on Thursdays at three o'clock, then *this is a sacred date* and nothing must get in the way. Unless the appointment becomes predictable by being reliable, the individual boy will not be able to make use of it, and of course one of the first ways in which he will make use of it if he begins to feel that it is reliable is to waste it. These things have to be accepted and tolerated. There is no need for anyone in this role of psychotherapist to be clever. All that is necessary is to be willing in the specialized time set aside to become involved with whatever is there in the child at the time or with whatever turns up through the patient's unconscious cooperation, which soon develops and which produces a powerful process. It is this process in the child that makes the sessions valuable.

Discussion

In the discussion that followed, a member asked the question: how among a lot of boys would one recognize one that could be chosen out of all the rest for this kind of special treatment? My answer, which had to be brief, was that probably one would choose a boy who has just boiled up into being especially difficult. This special clinical problem must either result in punishment and further hardening or else it can be used as a communication indicating a new hope.

The question is, what is this hope? What does the child hope to do? It is difficult to answer this question. The child, without knowing it, hopes to be able to take someone who will listen back to the moment of deprivation or to the phase in which deprivation became consolidated into an inescapable reality. The hope is that the boy or girl will be able to re-experience in relation to the person who is acting as psychotherapist the intense suffering that followed immediately the reaction to deprivation. The moment that the child has used the support that the therapist can give to reach back to the intense suffering of that fateful moment or period of time, there follows a memory of *the time before the deprivation*. In this way the child has reached back either to the lost capacity to find objects or to the lost security of the framework. The child has reached back to a creative relationship to external reality or to the period in which spontaneity was safe, even if it involved aggressive impulses. This time the reaching back has been done without stealing and without aggression, because it is something that happens automatically as a result of the child's arrival at what had previously been intolerable: the suffering reactive to the deprivation. By suffering I mean acute confusion, disintegration of the personality, falling for ever, a loss of contact with the body, complete disorientation and other states of this nature. Once one has taken a child to this area and the child has come through to remember it and what went before, then one has no difficulty whatever in understanding why it is that anti-social children must spend their lives looking for help of this kind. They cannot get on with their own lives until someone has gone back with them and enabled them to remember by reliving the immediate result of the deprivation.

[Dr Winnicott attempted to make his point clearer by giving as an example the beginning of an interview with a boy who was brought to him for stealing. This boy was lolling back in the chair set aside in his room for a parent. His father was behaving very well, as if doing it for the child, while the child was exploiting the situation and taking charge. Any attempt to make this boy behave himself would have put out of court the possibility that the hour might be used productively. Gradually the boy settled down to some kind of game. The father was able to go to the waiting room and then there followed a communication between the boy and the therapist of a deepening kind. At the end of an hour the boy had been able to remember and to describe with fullness of feeling the difficult moment that he had not been able to manage years ago when he had felt abandoned in a hospital.

This description was given in illustration of the way in which for the time being the person doing the psychotherapy must abandon everything that has to be used in the management of a group, although, of course, after the end of the allotted time there must be a return to the general attitude which makes the running of the group possible. Dr Winnicott repeated that he was not sure that in the Borstal groups it would be possible to combine general management with personal work, even with one or two of the individual boys at a time. Nevertheless, he felt that some interest might be obtained from an attempt to describe the inherent difficulties and also the possible rewards.

Varieties of Psychotherapy

*A talk given to MIASMA (Mental Illness
Association Social and Medical Aspects),
Cambridge, 6 March 1961*

You will more often hear discussed varieties of illness
than varieties of therapy. Naturally, the two are interrelated
and I shall need to talk about illness first and therapy later

I am a psychoanalyst, and you will not mind if I say that
the basis of psychotherapy is the psychoanalytic training.
This includes the personal analysis of the student analyst.
Apart from such a training, it is psychoanalytic theory and
psychoanalytic metapsychology that influence all dynamic
psychology, of whatever school.

There are, however, many varieties of psychotherapy,
and these should depend for their existence not on the
views of the practitioner, but on the need of the patient or
of the case. Let us say that, where possible, we advise
psychoanalysis, but where this is not possible or where
there are arguments against, then an appropriate modification may be devised.

Of the many patients who come to me one way or another,
only a very small percentage do in fact get psychoanalytic
treatment, although I work at the centre of the psychoanalytic
world.

I could talk about the technical modifications that are
called for when the patient is psychotic or borderline, but it
is not this that I wish to discuss here.

My special interest here is in the way in which a trained

analyst can do something other than analysis and do it usefully. This is important when, as is usual, a limited amount of time is available for treatment. Often these other treatments can look better than the treatments that I personally feel have a more profound effect, i.e. psychoanalysis.

First let me say that one essential of psychotherapy is that no other treatment shall be mixed up with it. It is not possible to do the work if the idea of a possible shock therapy is looming large, as this alters the whole clinical picture. The patient either fears or secretly longs for the physical treatment (or both), and the psychotherapist never meets the patient's real personal problem.

On the other hand, I must take for granted adequate physical care of the body.

The next thing is, what is our aim? Do we wish to do as much as possible or as little? In psychoanalysis we ask ourselves: how much can we do? At the other extreme, in my hospital clinic, our motto is: how little need we do? This makes us always aware of the economic aspect of the case; also, it makes us look for the central illness in a family, or for the social illness, so that we may avoid wasting our time and someone's money by giving treatments to the secondary characters in a family drama. There is nothing original in this, but you will perhaps like to hear a psychoanalyst say this, since analysts are especially liable to get bogged down in long treatments in the course of which they may lose sight of an adverse external factor.

And then, how much of the patient's difficulties belong simply to the fact that no one has ever intelligently listened? I very quickly discovered as long as forty years ago that the taking of case histories from mothers is in itself a psychotherapy if it be well done. Time must be allowed and a non-moralistic attitude naturally adopted, and when the mother has come to the end of saying what is in her mind, she may add: 'Now I understand how the present symptoms fit into the whole pattern of the child's life in the family, and I can manage now, simply because you let me get at the whole story in my own way and in my own time.' This is not only a matter that concerns parents who bring their children; adults say this about themselves, and psychoanalysis could be said to be one long, very long, history-taking.

You know, of course, of the transference in psychoanalysis. In the psychoanalytic setting patients bring samples of their past and of their inner reality and expose them in the fantasy that belongs to their ever-changing relationship to the analyst. In this way the unconscious can gradually be made conscious. Once this process has started up and the unconscious cooperation of the patient has been gained, there is always much to be done; hence the length of the average treatment. It is interesting to examine the first interviews. If a psychoanalytic treatment is starting, the analyst is careful not to be too clever at the beginning; and there is a good reason for this. The patient brings to the first interviews all his belief and all his suspicion. These extremes must be allowed to find real expression. If the analyst does too much at the beginning, the patient either runs away or else, out of fear, develops a most splendid belief and becomes almost as if hypnotized.

Before I go further I must mention some other assumptions. There can be no reserved area in the patient. Psychotherapy does not prescribe for a patient's religion, his cultural interest or his private life, but a patient who keeps part of himself completely defended is avoiding the dependence that is inherent in the process. You will see that this dependence carries with it a corresponding thing in the therapist, a professional reliability which is even more important than the reliability of the doctor in ordinary medical practice. It is interesting that the Hippocratic oath which founded the medical practice recognized this with crude clarity.

Again, by the theory that underlies all our work, a disorder that is not physically caused and that is therefore psychological represents a hitch in the individual's emotional development. Psychotherapy aims simply and solely at undoing the hitch, so that development may take place where formerly it could not.

In another, though parallel, language, psychological disorder is immaturity, immaturity of the emotional growth of the individual; and this growth includes the evolution of the individual's capacity to be related to people and to the environment generally.

In order to make myself clear I must give you a view of psychological disorder, of the categories of personal immaturity, even if this involves a gross simplification of a highly complex matter. I make three categories. The first of these brings to mind the term 'psychoneurosis'. Here are all the disorders of individuals who were well-enough cared for in the early stages to be in a position, developmentally, to meet and to fail, to some extent, to contain the difficulties that are inherent in the full life, a life in which the individual rides and is not ridden by the instincts. I must include in with this the more 'normal' varieties of depression.

The second of these categories brings to mind the word 'psychosis'. Here, something went wrong in the area of the very early details of infant nurture, the result being a disturbance of the basic structuring of the individual's personality. This basic fault, as Balint[1] has called it, may have produced an infantile or childhood psychosis, or difficulties at later stages may have exposed a fault in ego structure which had passed unnoticed. Patients in this category were never healthy enough to become psychoneurotic.

The third category I reserve for the in-betweens, those individuals who started well enough, but whose environment failed them at some point, or repeatedly, or over a long period of time. These are children or adolescents or adults who could rightly claim: 'All was well until . . . and my personal life cannot be developed unless the environment acknowledges its debt to me,' but of course it is not usual for the deprivation and the suffering it produces to be available to consciousness, so that instead of the words we find clinically an attitude, one which displays an antisocial tendency, and

1. M. Balint, *The Basic Fault*, London, Tavistock Publications, 1968.

which may crystallize into delinquency and into recidivism.

For the moment, then, you are looking at psychological illness through the wrong end of three telescopes. Through one telescope you see reactive depression, which has to do with the destructive urges that accompany loving impulses in two-body relationships (basically, infant and mother), and also you see psychoneurosis, which has to do with ambivalence, that is to say, coexisting love and hate, which belongs to triangular relationships (basically, child and two parents), the relationship being experienced both heterosexually and homosexually, in varying proportions.

Through the second telescope you see the very early stages of emotional development becoming distorted by faulty infant care. I admit that some infants are more difficult to nurture than others, but as we are not out to blame anyone, we can ascribe the cause of illness here to a failure in nurture. What we see is a failure of the structuring of the personal self, and the capacity of the self for relating to objects that are of the environment. I would like to dig this rich seam with you, but I must not do so.

Through this telescope we see the various failures which produce the clinical picture of schizophrenia, or which produce the psychotic undercurrents that disturb the even flow of life of many of us who manage to get labelled normal, healthy, mature.

When we look at illness in this way, we only see exaggerations of elements in our own selves; we do not see anything which would put psychiatrically ill people in a place apart. Hence the strain inherent in treating or in nursing ill people psychologically, rather than by drugs and by the so-called physical treatments.

The third telescope takes our attention away from the difficulties inherent in life to disturbances which have a different nature, for the deprived person is prevented from getting at his or her own inherent problems by a grudge, a justified claim for a mending of an almost remembered insult. We in this room are probably not in this category, not even slightly.

Most of us can say of our parents: 'They made mistakes, they constantly frustrated us, and it fell to their lot to introduce us to the Reality Principle, arch-enemy of spontaneity, creativity and the sense of Real, BUT they never really let us down.' It is this being let down that constitutes the basis for the anti-social tendency, and however much we dislike our bicycles being stolen, or having to use the police to prevent violence, we do see, we understand, why this boy or that girl forces us to meet a challenge, whether by stealing or by destructiveness.

I have done as much as I can allow myself to build up a theoretical background for my brief description of some varieties of psychotherapy.

Category 1: Psychoneurosis

If illness in this category needs treatment, we would like to provide psychoanalysis, a professional setting of general reliability in which the repressed unconscious may become conscious. This is brought about as a result of the appearance in the 'transference' of innumerable samples of the patient's personal conflicts. In a favourable case the defences against anxiety that arise out of the instinctual life and its imaginative elaboration become less and less rigid, and more and more under the patient's deliberate control system.

Category 2: Failure in Early Nurture

In so far as illness of this kind needs treatment, we need to provide opportunity for the patient to have experiences that properly belong to infancy under conditions of extreme dependence. We see that such conditions may be found apart from organized psychotherapy, for instance, in friendship, in nursing care that may be provided on account of physical illness, in cultural experiences, including for some those that are called religious. A family that continues to care for a child provides opportunities for regression to dependence even of a high order; and it is indeed a regular feature of family life, well embedded in a social milieu, this going on being available to re-establish and to emphasize elements of care that belong initially to infant care. You will agree that some children enjoy their families and their growing independence, while others continue to use their families psychotherapeutically.

Professional social work comes in here, as an attempt to give professionally the help which would be provided nonprofessionally by parents and by families and by social units. The social worker, on the whole, is not a psychotherapist in the sense described in Category 1. The social worker is a psychotherapist, however, in meeting Category 2 needs.

You will see that a great deal that a mother does with an infant could be called 'holding'. Not only is actual holding very important, and a delicate matter that can only be delicately done by the right people, but also much of infant nurture is an ever-widening interpretation of the word 'holding'. Holding comes to include all physical management, in so far as it is done in adaptation to an infant's needs. Gradually a child values being let go, and this corresponds with the presentation to the child of the Reality Principle, which at first clashes with the Pleasure Principle (omnipotence abrogated). The family continues this holding, and society holds the family.

Casework might be described as the professionalized aspect of this normal function of parents and of local social units, a 'holding' of persons and of situations, while growth tendencies are given a chance. These growth tendencies are present all the time in every individual, except where hopelessness (because of repeated environmental failure) has led to an organized withdrawal. The tendencies have been described in terms of integration, of the psyche coming to terms with the body, the one becoming linked with the other, and of the development of a capacity for relating to objects. These processes go ahead unless blocked by failures of holding and of the meeting of the individual's creative impulses.

Category 3: Deprivation

Where patients are dominated by a *deprivation* area in their past history, the treatment needs to be adapted to this fact. As persons they may be normal, neurotic or psychotic. One can hardly see what is the personal pattern, because whenever hope begins to become alive, the boy or girl produces a symptom (stealing or being stolen from, destructiveness or being destroyed) which forces the environment to notice and to act. Action is usually punitive, but what the patient needs, of course, is a full acknowledgement and full payment. As I have said, this very often cannot be done because so much is unavailable to consciousness, but it is important that a serious digging done in the early stages of an antisocial career quite frequently does produce the clue and the solution. A study of delinquency should be started as a study of the antisocial in relatively normal children whose homes are intact, and here I find it frequently possible to track down the deprivation and the extreme suffering that resulted and which altered the whole course of the child's development. (I have published cases, and I can give other examples if there is time.)[2]

The point here is that society is left with all the untreated and untreatable cases in which the antisocial tendency has built up into a stabilized delinquency. Here the need is for the provision of specialized environments, and these must be divided into two kinds:

1. Those which hope to socialize the children they are holding.

2. Those which are merely designed to keep their children in order to preserve society from them until these boys and girls are too old to be detained, and until they go out into the world as adults who will repeatedly get into trouble. This latter kind of institution may run most smoothly when very strictly administered.

Can it be seen that it is very dangerous to base a system of

2. Examples can be found in *Therapeutic Consultations in Child Psychiatry*, London, Hogarth Press, 1971. [Eds.]

child care on the work done in homes for the maladjusted, and especially on the 'successful' management of delinquents in detention centres?

On the basis of what I have said, it is now perhaps possible to compare the three types of psychotherapy.

Naturally, a practising psychiatrist needs to be able to pass easily from one kind of therapy to another, and indeed to do all kinds at one and the same time if necessary, as need arises.

Illness of psychotic quality (Category 2) demands of us that we organize a complex kind of 'holding', including, if necessary, physical care. Here the professional therapist or nurse comes in when the patient's immediate environment fails to cope. As a friend of mine (the late John Rickman) said, 'Insanity is not being able to find anyone to stand you,' and here there are two factors: the degree of illness in the patient and the ability of the environment to tolerate the symptoms. In this way there are some in the world who are more ill than some of those who are in mental hospitals.

Psychotherapy of the kind I am referring to can look like friendship, but it is not friendship because the therapist is paid and only sees the patient for a limited period by appointment, and, moreover, only over a limited course of time, since the aim in every therapy is to arrive at a point at which the professional relationship ends because the patient's life and living takes over and the therapist passes on to the next job.

A therapist is like other professional people in that in his job his behaviour is at a higher standard than it is in his private life. He is punctual, he adapts himself to his patient's needs, and he does not live out his own frustrated urges in his contact with his patients.

It will be evident that patients who are very ill in this category do put a very great strain on the integrity of the therapist, since they do need human contact, and real feelings, and yet they need to place an absolute reliance on the relationship in which they are maximally dependent. The greatest difficulties come when there has been a seduction in the patient's childhood, in which case there must be ex-

perienced in the course of the treatment a delusion that the
therapist is repeating seduction. Naturally, recovery depends
on the undoing of this childhood seduction, which brought
the child prematurely to a real, instead of an imaginary, sexual
life, and spoiled the child's perquisite: unlimited play.

In therapy designed to deal with psychoneurotic illness
(Category 1), the classical psychoanalytic setting devised by
Freud can be easily attained, since the patient brings to the
treatment a degree of belief and a capacity to trust. With all
this taken for granted, the analyst has the opportunity to
allow the transference to develop in its own way, and instead
of the patient's delusions, there come into the material of the
analysis dreams, imagination and ideas expressed in symbolic
form which can be interpreted according to the process as it
develops through the unconscious cooperation of the patient.

This is all I have time to say about the psychoanalytic
technique, which can be learned, and which is difficult
enough, but not as exhausting as therapy designed to meet
psychotic disorder.

Psychotherapy designed to deal with an antisocial tendency
in a patient only works, as I have said, if the patient is near
the beginning of his or her antisocial career, before secondary
gains and delinquent skills have become established. It is
only in the early stages that the patient knows he (or she) is a
patient, and actually feels a need to get to the roots of the
disturbance. Where work is possible along these lines, the
doctor and the patient settle down to a sort of detective story,
using any clues that may be available, including what is
known of the past history of the case, and the work is done in
a thin layer that is somewhere between the deeply buried
unconscious and the conscious life and memory system of
the patient.

This layer that is between the unconscious and the conscious is occupied in normal people by cultural pursuits. The
cultural life of the delinquent is notoriously thin, because
there is no freedom in such a case except in a flight either to
the unremembered dream or to reality. Any attempt to ex-

plore the intermediate area leads not to art or religion or playing, but to antisocial behaviour that is compulsive and inherently unrewarding to the individual, as well as hurtful to society.

Cure

A talk given to doctors and nurses in St Luke's Church, Hatfield, on St Luke's Sunday, 18 October 1970

Using this opportunity that I have been offered, I wish to try to verbalize some of the thoughts and feelings that I imagine are common to us all.

I do not deal with the religion of inner experience, which is not my special line, but I deal with the philosophy of our work as medical practitioners, a kind of religion of external relationship.

There is this good word in our language: CURE. If this word be allowed to talk, it can be expected to tell a story. Words have that kind of value, they have etymological roots, they have a history: like human beings, they have a struggle sometimes to establish and maintain identity.

At a most superficial level, the word 'cure' points to a common denominator in religious and medical practice. I believe cure at its roots means care. About 1700 it started to degenerate into a name for medical treatment, as in water-cure. Another century gave it the added implication of successful outcome; the patient is restored to health, the disease is destroyed, the evil spirit is exorcized.

The lines

> Let the water and the blood
> Be of sin the double cure

contain already more than a hint of the passage from care to remedy, the transition that I am looking at here and now.

In medical practice there is to be found a gap between the two extremes in the use of the word. Cure, in the sense of remedy, successful eradication of disease and its cause, tends today to overlay cure as care. Medical practitioners are all the time engaged in a battle to prevent the two meanings of the word from losing touch with each other. The general practitioner, it might be said, cares, but must know about remedies. By contrast, the specialist is caught up in problems of diagnosis and the eradication of disease, and what he must make an effort to remember is this: that care also belongs to medical practice. At the first of these two extreme positions the doctor is a social worker and is almost fishing in the pools that provide proper angling for the curate, the minister of religion. At the other extreme position the doctor is a technician, both in making a diagnosis and in treating.

The field is so vast that specialization one way or another is inevitable. Nevertheless, as thinkers we are not exonerated from the attempt on a holistic approach.

What do people want of us as doctors and nurses, what do we want of our colleagues when it is we ourselves who are immature, ill or old? These conditions – immaturity, illness, old age – carry with them the fact of dependence. It follows that what is needed is dependability. As doctors, and also as nurses and social workers, we are called upon to be humanly (not mechanically) reliable, to have reliability built into our overall attitude. (For the moment I must assume that we have a capacity to recognize dependence and to adapt to what we find.)

There is no dispute about the value of effectual remedy. (I owe the fact that I am not a cripple, and my wife owes her life, for instance, to penicillin.) Applied science in medical and surgical practice is to be taken for granted. We are unlikely to undervalue the specific remedy. From an acceptance of this principle, however, it is possible for the observer and the thinker to proceed to other considerations.

Reliability meeting dependence is the theme of this talk. It will become quickly evident that the theme leads on to infinite complexities, so that artificial boundaries will need to be set up to delineate areas for discussion.

Immediately you will see that this way of talking separates the doctor practising in his own right from the doctor who acts for society.

If I criticize the medical profession, it should be stated that I have been proud to have been a member of that profession ever since I became licensed fifty years ago, and I have never wanted to be anything else but a doctor. This fact does not stop me from seeing glaring faults in our attitudes and social claims, and I assure you I know all about the beam in mine own eye.

Perhaps it is when we are patients that we most easily see the faults in our colleagues, and alongside this we may place the fact that we know what we owe to the medical and nursing professions best when we have been ill and have recovered.

I am not, of course, referring to mistakes. I personally have made mistakes that I hate to think about. Once, before the days of insulin, I drowned a diabetic patient in a stupid and ignorant attempt to apply instructions from above. The fact that the man would have died anyway does not make me feel better. And I have done worse things. Happy is the young doctor who does not get exposed as ignorant before he has built up some position among colleagues that will see him through disasters. But all this is treading well-worn paths. We accept fallibility as a fact of human endearment.

I wish to look at the way you and I practise medicine and surgery and nursing, *when we are doing well*, and not building up material for remorse.

How can I choose? It is necessary for me to call on the experience I have had of a specialized kind, that is, in my practice of psychoanalysis and of child psychiatry. I suggest that there is a great deal of potential feedback from psychiatric to medical practice. Psychoanalysis is not just a matter of interpreting the repressed unconscious; it is rather the provision of a professional setting for trust, in which such work may take place.

I personally turned over gradually from being a physician to children and their parents to being a psychoanalyst. Psychoanalysis (like analytical psychology) is linked to a theory and to the intensive training of a few self-elected and selected individuals. The training aims at providing psychotherapy that reaches to unconscious motivation, and that essentially makes use of what is called 'transference'. And so on.

I will enunciate certain principles that emerge from the sort of work that my colleagues and I find ourselves doing. I have chosen seven descriptive categories:

1. Hierarchies.
2. Who is ill? Dependence.
3. Effect on us of care-cure position.
4. Further effects.
5. Gratitude/propitiation.
6. Holding. Facilitation. Individual growth.

1. First, the matter of hierarchies. We find that when we are face to face with a man, woman or child in our speciality, we are reduced to two human beings of equal status. Hierarchies drop away. I may be a doctor, a nurse, a social worker, a residential houseparent – or, for that matter, I may be a psychoanalyst or a parson. It makes no difference. What is significant is the interpersonal relationship in all its rich and complex human colours.

There is a place for hierarchies in the social structure, but not in clinical confrontation.

2. From here it is a short step to the question: which of the two is ill? Sometimes it is a matter of convenience. It is valuable to understand that the concept of illness and of being ill brings immediate relief, because it legitimizes dependence, and the one who succeeds in the claim to be ill benefits in a specific way. 'You are ill' naturally moves me into the position of one who responds to need, that is to say,

of adaptation, concern and reliability, of cure in the sense of *care*. The doctor or nurse or whoever it be moves naturally into a professional attitude to the patient. This carries no sense of superiority.

Which of the two would it be? One could almost say that the assumption of the cure position is also an illness, only it is the other side of the coin. We need our patients as much as they need us. The Provost of Derby recently quoted from St Vincent de Paul, who said to his followers, 'Pray that the poor may forgive us for helping them.' We could pray that the ill forgive us for responding to their illness needs. We are talking about love, but if love is to be provided by professionals in a professional setting, then the meaning of the word must be spelt out. In this century it is the psychoanalysts who are doing the spelling out.

3. We can now look at the effect that this assumption of the role of one who cares has on us ourselves, who care for, and who care-cure. We note five main things:

(a) In the role of care-curers we are non-moralistic. It does not help a patient to tell him or her that he or she is wicked to be ill. Nor does it help a thief, or a person with asthma, or a schizophrenic to be put into a moralistic category. The patient knows we are not there to judge him.

(b) We are dead-honest, truthful, saying we do not know when we do not know. An ill person cannot stand our fear of the truth. If we fear the truth, let us take up another profession, not that of doctor.

(c) We become reliable in the way that we can only sustain in our professional work. The point is that by being reliable persons (professionally) we protect our patients from the unpredictable. Many of them suffer from precisely this, that they have been subjected as part of the pattern of their lives to the unpredictable. We cannot afford to fit into this pattern. Behind unpredictability lies mental confusion, and behind that there can be found chaos in terms of somatic functioning, i.e. unthinkable anxiety that is physical.

(*d*) We accept the patient's love and hate, are affected by it, but we do not provoke either, nor do we hope to gain in a professional relationship emotional satisfactions (loving or hating) that ought to be worked out in our private lives and in the realms of the personal or else in the inner psychic reality, when dreaming takes shape and assumes shapes. (In psychoanalysis, this is studied as an essential factor, and the name 'transference' is given to the specific dependencies that arise between patient and analyst. The doctor who is involved in physical medicine and surgery has much to learn from psychoanalysis, in this area especially. To take up a very simple point: *if a doctor appears at the time arranged, he experiences a tremendous strengthening of the patient's trust in him* (*or her*), and this is not only important for the avoidance of patient agony, but also it enhances the somatic processes tending towards healing, even of tissues, certainly of functions.)

(*e*) We assume and easily agree to assume that the doctor or nurse is not being cruel for the sake of being cruel. Cruelty comes into our work, inevitably, but for *cruelty indulgence* we must look to life itself outside our professional relationships. And there is no room for vindictiveness in our professional work. I could, of course, tell of cruelty and vindictiveness practised by doctors, but we would find no difficulty here in putting this sort of malpraxis in its place.

4. To reach to further effects on us of our recognizing the illness and therefore the dependence needs of our patients, we must consider more complex matters of personality structure. For instance, a sign of health in the mind is the ability of one individual to enter imaginatively and yet accurately into the thoughts and feelings and hopes and fears of another person; also to allow the other person to do the same to us. I suppose that care-curing parsons and doctors, by self-selection, are good at this sort of thing. But exorcists and remedy-curers do not need it.

It may sometimes be a burden to be able to play too well

with cross-identifications. Yet somehow, in selection of medical students, surely one of the important features (if this could be tested) would be an assessment of the capacity for what I am calling cross-identifications, standing in the other person's shoes, and allowing the converse. There can be little doubt that cross-identifications greatly enrich all human experiences, and that those who have but a poor capacity in this respect find themselves bored, and are boring to others. Moreover, they cannot get far beyond the technician-type function in medical practice, and they can cause much suffering without knowing it. James Baldwin, speaking recently on the BBC, mentioned the sin the Christians forgot to mention: the sin of unawareness. I could add a note here on delusional cross-identifications. These cause havoc indeed.

5. Next I come back to the matter <u>of gratitude</u>. I referred to this in giving the quotation from St Vincent de Paul. Gratitude looks very nice, and we like the odd bottle of whisky and box of chocolates that are expressions of thanks from patients. Nevertheless, gratitude is not as simple as all that. If things go well, patients take the going well for granted, and it is only if there is neglect (a swab left in the peritoneum) that they become true to themselves and complain. In other words, most gratitude, certainly exaggerated gratitude, is a matter of propitiation; there are avenging forces latent, and they had better be appeased.

Ill people lie in bed planning generous gifts or codicils to wills, but doctors and nurses and others are pleased that after discharge the sad patient soon forgets, though perhaps is not forgotten. I would claim that it is doctors and nurses who experience reduplicated and repetitive mourning; one of the hazards of our professional life is that we may become hardened, because the repeated losses of patients make us wary against getting fond of the newly ill. This is especially true of nurses who care for sick babies, or who take over the care of babies who are left in telephone kiosks, or are found (like Ernest) in a handbag at the Victoria Station Lost Property Office.

General practice in a country district may be the answer to this problem, because the doctor lives among his patients – surely the best kind of doctoring. The doctor and the patient, each always there, but only at times doctor and patient.

There is a very great deal for the practising doctor to learn from those who specialize in care-cure, rather than in cure to eradicate evil agencies.

6. There is one thing especially that needs to feed back into medical practice, and I will end with this. It is that care-cure is an extension of the concept of holding. It starts with the baby in the womb, then with the baby in arms, and enrichment comes from the growth process in the infant, which the mother makes possible because of her knowing just what it is like to be this one particular baby that she has given birth to.

The theme of the facilitating environment enabling personal growth and the maturational process has to be a description of father–mother care, and of the family function, and this leads on to the whole build-up of democracy as a political extension of family facilitation, with the mature individuals eventually taking part according to their age and capacity in politics and in the maintenance and rebuilding of the political structure.

Along with this is the sense of personal identity which is essential for every human being, and which *can only become fact in each individual case because of good-enough mothering* and environmental provision of the holding variety at the stages of immaturity. The maturational process alone cannot take the individual through to his or her becoming an individual.

So when I speak of cure in the sense of care-cure, here is the doctors' and the nurses' natural tendency to meet the dependence of ill patients, but now this is spelt out in terms of health: it is written down in terms of the natural dependence of the immature individual, which calls out in parent-figures a tendency to provide conditions that foster individual growth. This is not cure, in the sense of remedy, so much as care-cure, the subject of my talk, and it could be the motto of our profession.

In terms of society's sickness, the care-cure may be of more importance in the world even than remedy-cure, and all the diagnosis and prevention that goes with what is usually called a scientific approach.

Here we are at one with social workers, whose term 'casework' can be looked at as a highly complex extension of the use of the word 'holding' and as a practical application of care-cure.

In a professional setting, given appropriate professional behaviour, the ill patient may find a personal solution to complex problems of the emotional life and of interpersonal relationships; and what we have done is to facilitate growth, not to apply a remedy.

Is care-cure too much to ask of the clinician? This aspect of our work seems to fail in terms of the claim for higher fees, and it undermines the status system of accepted hierarchies. Nevertheless, it can easily be learned by suitable persons, and it brings something much more satisfying than the feeling of having been clever.

I suggest that we find in the care-cure aspect of our professional work a setting for the application of principles that we learned at the beginning of our lives, when as immature persons we were given good-enough care, and cure, so to speak, in advance (the best kind of preventive medicine) by our 'good-enough' mothers, and by our parents.

It is always a steadying thing to find that one's work links with entirely natural phenomena, and with the universals, and with what we expect to find in the best of poetry, philosophy and religion.

Part 2

The Family

The Mother's Contribution to Society

The postscript to Dr Winnicott's first collection of broadcast talks, published under the title The Child and the Family, *1957*

I suppose that everyone has a paramount interest, a deep, driving propulsion towards something. If one's life lasts long enough, so that looking back becomes allowable, one discerns an urgent tendency that has integrated all the various and varied activities of one's private life and one's professional career.

As for me, I can already see what a big part has been played in my work by the urge to find and to appreciate the ordinary good mother. Fathers, I know, are just as important, and indeed an interest in mothering includes an interest in fathers, and in the vital part they play in child care. But for me it has been to mothers that I have so deeply needed to speak.

It seems to me that there is something missing in human society. Children grow up and become in their turn fathers and mothers, but, on the whole, they do not grow up to know and acknowledge just what their mothers did for them at the start. The reason is that the part the mother plays has only recently begun to be perceived. But here I must make something clear; there are certain things I do not mean.

I do not mean that children should thank their parents for conceiving them. Surely they may hope that the original coming together was a matter of mutual pleasure and satisfaction. Parents certainly cannot expect thanks for the fact of a child's existence. Babies do not ask to be born.

There are other things I do not mean. For instance, I do not mean that children are under any obligation to their fathers and mothers at all on account of their cooperation in home-building and family affairs, even though gratitude may eventually develop. Ordinary good parents do build a home and stick together, thus providing the basic ration of child care and thus maintaining a setting in which each child can gradually find the self and the world, and a working relationship between the two. But parents do not want gratitude for this; they get their rewards, and rather than be thanked they prefer to see their children growing up and themselves becoming parents and home-builders. This can be put the other way round. Boys and girls can legitimately blame parents when, after bringing about their existence, they do not furnish them with that start in life which is their due.

In the last half century there has been a great increase in awareness of the value of the home. (It cannot be helped if this awareness came first out of an understanding of the effect of the bad home.) We know something of the reasons why this long and exacting task, the parents' job of seeing their children through, is a job worth doing; and, in fact, we believe that it provides the only real basis for society, and the only factory for the democratic tendency in a country's social system.

But the home is the parents', not the child's, responsibility. I want to be very clear that I am not asking any one to be expressing gratitude. What particularly concerns me neither goes back so far as conception nor is it as far forward as home-building. I am concerned with the mother's relation to her baby just before the birth and in the first weeks and months after the birth. I am trying to draw attention to the immense contribution to the individual and to society that the ordinary good mother with her husband in support makes at the beginning, and which she does simply through being devoted to her infant.

Is not this contribution of the devoted mother unrecognized precisely because it is immense? If this contribution is accepted, it follows that every man or woman who is sane, every man or woman who has the feeling of being a person in the world, and for whom the world means something, every happy person, is in infinite debt to a woman. At the time when as an infant (male or female) this person knew nothing about dependence, there was absolute dependence.

Once again, let me emphasize, the result of such recognition when it comes will not be gratitude or even praise. The result will be a lessening in ourselves of a fear. If our society delays making full acknowledgement of this dependence, which is a historical fact in the initial stage of development of every individual, there must remain a block both to progress and to regression, a block that is based on fear. If there is no true recognition of the mother's part, then there must remain a vague fear of dependence. This fear will sometimes take the form of a fear of WOMAN, or fear of a woman, and at other times will take less easily recognized forms, always including the fear of domination.

Unfortunately, the fear of domination does not lead groups of people to avoid being dominated; on the contrary, it draws them towards a specific or chosen domination. Indeed, were the psychology of the dictator studied, one would expect to find that, amongst other things, he in his own personal struggle is trying to control the woman whose domination he unconsciously fears, trying to control her by encompassing her, acting for her, and in turn demanding total subjection and 'love'.

Many students of social history have thought that fear of WOMAN is a powerful cause of the seemingly illogical behaviour of human beings in groups, but this fear is seldom traced to its root. Traced to its root in the history of each individual, this fear of WOMAN turns out to be a fear of recognizing the fact of dependence. There are therefore good social reasons for instigating research into the very early stages of the infant–mother relationship.

For my part, I happen to have been drawn towards finding out all I can about the meaning of the word 'devotion', and towards being able, if possible, to make a fully informed and fully felt acknowledgement to my own mother. Here a man is in a more difficult position than a woman; he obviously cannot come to terms with his mother by becoming a mother, in turn, and in due course. He has no alternative but to go as far as he can towards a consciousness of the mother's achievement. The development of motherliness as a quality in his character does not get far enough, and femininity in a man proves to be a side-track to the main issues.

One solution for a man caught up in this problem is to take part in an objective study of the mother's part, especially the part she plays at the beginning.

At present, the importance of the mother at the start is often denied, and instead it is said that in the early months it is only a technique of bodily care that is needed, and that therefore a good nurse will do just as well. We even find mothers (not, I hope, in this country) being told that they *must mother* their infants, this being the most extreme degree of denial that 'mothering' grows naturally out of being a mother. It often happens that just before an understanding of some matter, there is a stage of denial, or blindness, or deliberate not seeing, just as the sea withdraws from the sands before throwing forward the thundering wave.

Administrative tidiness, the dictates of hygiene, a laudable urge towards the promotion of bodily health – these and all sorts of other things get between the mother and her baby, and it is unlikely that mothers themselves will rise up in concerted effort to protest against interference. Someone must act for the young mothers who are having their first and second babies, and who are necessarily themselves in a dependent state. It can be assumed that no mother of a new-born baby will ever go on strike against doctors and nurses, however much frustration exists, because she is otherwise engaged.

Though many of my broadcast talks are directed to

mothers, the young mothers who are chiefly concerned are unlikely to read them. I have no wish to alter this. I cannot assume that young mothers will ever want to know what it is that they do when they find that they enjoy minding their own infants. They naturally fear lest instruction shall spoil their enjoyment and their creative experience, which is the essential element leading to satisfaction and growth. The young mother needs protection and information, and she needs the best that medical science can offer in the way of bodily care, and prevention of avoidable accidents. She needs a doctor and a nurse whom she knows, and in whom she has confidence. She also needs the devotion of a husband, and satisfying sexual experiences. No, the young mother is not usually a learner from books. Nevertheless, in preparing broadcasts for publication I have kept to the form of direct talk with young mothers for the reason that this provides a discipline. A writer on human nature needs to be constantly drawn towards simple English and away from the jargon of the psychologist, valuable as this jargon may be in con-tributions to scientific journals.

Probably some who have already been through the mother-ing experience, and who therefore can afford to have a look round, will be interested to read what is said in this way, and they may be able to help to do what is so much needed at the present time, that is to say, to give moral support to the ordinary good mother, educated or uneducated, clever or limited, rich or poor, and to protect her from everyone and everything that gets between her baby and herself. We all join forces in enabling the emotional relationship between the mother and her new baby to start and to develop naturally. This collective task is an extension of the job of the father, of the father's job at the beginning, at the time when his wife is carrying, bearing and suckling his infant; in the period before the infant can make use of him in other ways.

The Child in the Family Group

*A talk given to the Nursery School Association
Conference on 'Developments in Primary
Education', held at New College, Oxford, 26
July 1966*

A great deal has been written recently on the subject
of the child and the family, and it is very difficult to know
how to contribute to this vast subject in an original way. It
must be the general feeling that everything has been said and
one can almost claim that the title has become meaningless
simply through repeated use. A little refreshment has come
recently through a change of emphasis in the directives, so
that now the accent is to be not on the individual, but on the
family. There is some sort of plan to change the pattern of
social work so that it is the family that is under consideration
and the child is thought of as part of the family.

In my opinion this means no change at all, because the
child has always been studied in relationship to the family or
to the lack of a family. But at any rate we can try to make use
of anything which relieves monotony. I do think that if we
look at the psychoanalytic contribution we can say that the
emphasis which psychoanalysts have placed on the treatment
of a child has been unbalanced. Psychoanalysis has been
through a long phase of discussing the treatment of one child
as a phenomenon seen in isolation. This could not be helped.
Within psychoanalytic circles there is a change here, however
– a change that has come simply through the processes of
development of ideas. The recent change in directive, how-

ever, is not aimed at the psychoanalyst. It is aimed at social work in general, and I would say that social work has always looked at the family when looking at the child.

There is a danger in my mind of an over-emphasis now of the management of human difficulties in terms of family and other groups as an escape from the study of the individual, whether child, infant, adolescent or grown-up. Somewhere or other in the work involved in every case, a caseworker must meet an individual out of the grouping; it is here that the biggest difficulties lie, and also it is here that there is the greatest potential for bringing about change.

I start, therefore, with a plea: remember the individual child, and the child's developmental process, and the child's distress, and the child's need for personal help, and the child's ability to make use of personal help, while of course remembering the importance of the family and the various school groups and all the other groups that lead on to the one that we call society.

In any piece of casework a decision has to be made on who is the ill person in this case. And sometimes, although it is the child that is put forward as ill, it is someone else who is causing and maintaining a disturbance, or it may even be that a social factor is the trouble. These are special cases and social workers are fully aware of this problem, which should not blind them, however, to the fact that in the vast majority of cases, when a child shows symptoms, these symptoms point to distress in the child which can best be met by work done with the child.

I want to remind you that this is especially true in all the myriad cases that exist in the community, but that do not get to the Child Guidance Clinics, which of course tend to find themselves dealing with the much less common, more complex cases. In other words, if you look around at the children that you know in your family and social setting, you will see a vast number of children who could do with a bit of help but who will never get to a clinic. I am saying that these are the children who can be helped best and who need individual attention. The children in the clinics are not representative of the children who are in need of help in the community. I say this with confidence to this audience because it is composed of teachers, and the majority of children that you teach are not clinic cases; they are the ordinary children, or much like those who belong to your social group. There is practically no child that is not in need of help over some personal problem, yesterday, today and tomorrow. Very often you deal with these problems in the school by ignoring them or by carefully graded discipline or by teaching the child a skill or by giving opportunity for creative impulses. And it has to be admitted that, on the whole, your view of psychology must be and must remain different from the views of the social worker and of the child psychiatrist.

You will understand that there must be an overlap and that some of your children ought to be attending a clinic and some of the clinic children ought to be dealing with their difficulties with the help of aunts and uncles and school teachers and every other kind of generalized social provision.

The Group in Relation to the Individual

What I want to do in order to make use of the opportunity you have given me is to remind you in some detail of the way in which the family is a group whose structure is related to the structure of the individual personality. The family is the first grouping, and of all groupings it is the one which is the nearest to being a grouping within the unit personality. The first grouping is simply a reduplication of the unit structure. When we say that the family is the first grouping, we are quite naturally talking in terms of the growth of the individual, and this is justified by the fact that the mere passage of time has no link with human living that is comparable in strength to the link that belongs to the fact that at a certain point in time each person starts and by a growth process makes an area of time personal.

The child is beginning to separate out from the mother,

and before the mother becomes objectively perceived, she is what might be called a subjective object. There is quite a jerk that the child has to experience between the use of a mother as a subjective object, that is to say an aspect of the self, and an object that is other than self and therefore outside omnipotent control; and the mother performs a most important task in adapting herself to the child's needs so that she blurs a little this terrible jerk to which I have referred and which belongs to meeting the Reality Principle. The mother-figure becomes reduplicated.

In some cultures a deliberate effort is made to prevent the mother from ever becoming one person, so that the child is ensured from the beginning against shock associated with loss. In our culture we tend to regard it as normal for the child to experience the full extent of the shock as the mother becomes an adaptive external person, but we have to admit that there are casualties. When it works with one mother, there is a richness of experience which is the main argument in its favour. Anthropological study of this area provides fascinating material for the research worker observing the results of the early and deliberate splitting of the mother-figure, socially determined.

The father comes into the picture in two ways. To some extent he is one of the people reduplicating the mother-figure, and there has been a change in orientation in this country in the last fifty years so that fathers become real to their infants much more in the role of reduplications of mother than they did, it would seem, a few decades ago. Nevertheless, it interferes with the other thing about a father, which is that he enters into the child's life as an aspect of the mother which is hard and strict and unrelenting, intransigent, indestructible, and which, under favourable circumstances, gradually becomes that man who turns out to be a human being, someone who can be feared and hated and loved and respected.

In this way a group has developed and we have to see that the group has come about in two sets of ways. The first set simply belongs to the extension of the child's personality structure and depends on growth processes. The other set depends on the mother and what she is like in her attitude to this particular child; on the other people who may be available as mother-figures; on the attitude of the mother to the surrogate mothers; on the social attitude in the locality; and then on the balance of the two aspects which I have described of the father-figure. What the father is like naturally very much determines the way in which the child uses or does not use him in the formation of this particular child's family. In any case, of course, the father may be absent or may be very much in evidence, and these details make a tremendous difference to the meaning of the word 'family' for the particular child we happen to be talking about.

Incidentally, I know of one child who gave the name 'Family' to her transitional object. I think that in this case there was a very early recognition of inadequacy in the parental relationship, and it was at an astonishingly early date that this child tried to remedy the deficiency that she perceived by calling her doll Family. It is the only instance I know in which this happened, and now thirty years later the person is still struggling with an inability to accept the estrangement between her parents.

What I hope to have done so far is to remind you that when we simply talk about a child and his or her family, we are ignoring the tricky stages in which that particular child acquired a family. It is not simply that there is a father and mother and that perhaps new children come along and then there is a home with parents and children enriched by aunts and uncles and cousins. This is just an observer's statement. For the five children in a family there are five families. It does not require a psychoanalyst to see that these five families need not resemble each other, and are certainly not identical.

The Reality Principle

Now that I have introduced the idea of a family along with the concept of the subjective object turning into one that is objectively perceived, I would like to continue a study in this area. There is an astonishingly big change that comes in the development of human beings just here between these two types of relationship. I personally have tried to contribute by making the most of our observations of transitional objects and transitional phenomena, that is to say, all the things employed by the individual child while he or she is passing through this phase in which there is a limited ability to make objective perceptions, and where the main experience of object-relating must continue to be relating to subjective objects. (Incidentally, it is not possible to use the words 'internal object' here; the object which we can see is external and is subjectively perceived, that is to say, it comes out of the creative impulses of the child and out of the child's mind. It is a more sophisticated matter when the child, now with an inside, takes externally perceived objects in and sets them up as internal images. We are discussing a stage before this language makes sense.)

A difficulty that presents itself in a description of this kind is that when a small child in this stage relates to what I am calling a subjective object, there is no doubt that at the same time there is objective perception at work. In other words, the child could not have invented exactly what the mother's left ear looks like. And yet in this stage one must say that the mother's left ear that the child is playing with is a subjective object; the child reached out and created that particular ear that happened to be there to be discovered. This is the exciting thing about the curtain in a theatre. When it goes up, each one of us will create the play that is going to be enacted, and afterwards we may even find that the overlap of what we have created, each one of us, provides material for a discussion about the play that was enacted.

I do not know how to go any further without saying that

there is an element of cheating somewhere here, cheating which is inherent in the individual's development of the capacity to relate to objects. I am reading this paper to you, to an audience that I have created. But it must be admitted that in writing the paper I have also to some extent thought about the audience that in fact is here now. I would like to think that this audience that is here now can join up to some extent with the audience that I had in mind when I was writing the paper, but there is no guarantee that the two audiences will be able to relate to each other. In writing this paper I have to play and I play about in the area which I call transitional, in which I am pretending that my audience is yourselves as you are here and now.

This phase that I am choosing to discuss and to which I have sometimes referred by using the term 'transitional phenomena' is important in the development of every individual child. Time is required within an 'average expectable environment'[1] so that the child may be helped by someone adapting in an extremely sensitive way while the child is in the process of acquiring a capacity to use fantasy, to call on inner reality and dream, and to manipulate toys. In playing, the child enters this intermediate area of what I am calling cheating, although I want to make it clear that just in this particular aspect of cheating there is health. The child uses a position in between himself or herself and the mother or father, whoever it is, and there whatever happens is symbolic of the union or the non-separation of these two separate things. The concept is really quite a difficult one and I think it would make a difference to philosophy if this could be grasped. It would also perhaps put religion once more into the experience of those who in fact have grown up out of the concept of miracles.

For our purpose here, the point is that the child requires a length of time in which steady experiences in relationships

1. This phrase was borrowed from Heinz Hartmann (see H. Hartmann, *Ego Psychology and the Problem of Adaptation*, 1939). [Eds.]

can be used for the development of intermediate areas in which transitional or play phenomena can become established for that particular child, established so that henceforward the child may enjoy all that is to be derived from the use of the symbol, for the symbol of union gives wider scope for human experience than union itself.

Excursions and Returns

I repeat that in healthy development the child needs *time* for this phase to be fully exploited, and here I am adding that the child needs to be able to experience the various kinds of object-relating all in the same day or even at one moment; for instance, you may see a small child enjoying relationships with an aunt or a dog or a butterfly and the observer may see not only that the child is making objective perceptions, but is enjoying the enrichment that comes from discovery. This does not mean, however, that the child is ready to live in a discovered world. At any moment the child merges in again with the cot or the mother or the familiar smells and is re-established in a subjective environment. What I am trying to say is that it is the child's family pattern more than any-thing else that supplies the child with these relics of the past, so that when the child discovers the world there is always the return journey that makes sense. If it is the child's own family, then the return journey does not put a strain on anyone, because it is of the essence of the family that it remains orientated to itself and to the people within it.

Although these points do not require illustrations I will take an incident from an analytic case.

> A woman patient sums up the accumulated traumata of her childhood by relating one incident in the way that patients often do. In her own words she shows the im-portance of the time factor. 'I was about two. The family was on the beach. I wandered away from mother and began to make discoveries. I found seashells. One seashell led me

on to another and there was an unlimited number. Suddenly I became frightened and I can see now that what had happened was that I had become interested in discovering the world and had forgotten mother. This carried with it, as I see now, the idea that mother had forgotten me. I therefore turned round and rushed back to mother, perhaps only a few yards. Mother took me up and a process started up of re-establishment of my relationship with her. I probably seemed uninterested in her because of this fact that time is required for me to feel re-established and to lose the sense of panic. Then suddenly mother put me down.'

This patient was in analysis and re-enacting this episode, and from the work done in the analysis she could add: 'Now I know what happened. I have been waiting all my life till now to be able to reach the next stage because if mother had not put me down I would have thrown my arms round her neck and have burst into a flood of tears, tears of joy and happiness. As it was, I never found my mother again.'

It will be understood that in giving this incident, the patient was referring to a pattern of this kind of situation based on superimposed memories of similar situations. The point about this illustration is that it shows the very delicate way in which, when all goes well, the child's confidence in the return journey is built up. This is a theme which is brought out in the three volumes, and especially the last, of Richard Church's autobiography.

In observing a child of two we can easily see the coexistence of excursions and return journeys that carry with them but little risk, and excursions and returns that are significant in that if they fail, they alter the child's whole life. Various members of the family have various parts to play and children use each other in extending their experiences to cover a wide field in the quality of excursions and returns.

In this way it often happens that a child at school is very different from a child at home. The more usual pattern is for the child at school to be excited in the discovery of new things, new aspects of reality newly perceived, while at the same time at home the child is conservative, withdrawn, dependent, near to panic, preserved from crisis by the sensitive adaptation of the mother or some other near person. It can be the other way round, but it is perhaps less normal and therefore more likely to give rise to difficulty when the child is full of confidence at school in relation to some one person, or to the setting, and at home is irritable, uncertain and prematurely independent. This could happen when there is no place in the family for the child to be, as when a second child has become the middle one of three children so that he or she has lost on all counts until someone notices that the child has altered in temperament and that, although in a good family, the child has become a deprived child.

Loyalty and Disloyalty

I would like to make a further development of the theme of the family as related to the theme of the developing individual. Of the many aspects of this phenomenon, which has so many facets, I would choose to speak of the conflicts of loyalty which are inherent in child development.

In its simplest terms, the problem can be stated in this way. There is a very great difference between a child who has walked away from the mother and reached the father and who has made the return journey, and a child who has never had this experience.

In more sophisticated language, the child is not equipped in the early stages for containing conflict within the self. This is something which we ask of the social worker, and we know what a strain it puts on mature adults when they do casework and over a period of time contain the conflicts that are inherent in a case. The caseworker puts more importance on this containment of the case than on any specific actions related to individuals in the group that comprises the case.

We must expect the immature child to need a situation in which loyalty is not expected, and it is in the family that we may hope to find this tolerance of what looks like disloyalty if it is not simply a part of the growth process.

A child moves over to a relationship to the father, and in doing so develops an attitude to the mother which belongs to relating to the father. Not only can the mother be seen objectively from where the father is, but also the child develops an in-love type of relationship to the father which involves hate of the mother and fear of the mother. It is dangerous to go back to the mother from this position. There has been a gradual build-up, however, and the child returns to the mother and in this familiar orientation sees the father objectively and the feelings of the child contain hate and fear.

This sort of thing goes on as a to-and-fro experience in the daily life of the child in the home. Of course, it need not be the father–mother relationship; it can be an experience of going from the mother to the nurse and back again, or it may be an aunt or a grandmother or a big sister. Gradually in the family all these possibilities can be met with, and experienced, and a child can come to terms with the fears associated with them. Moreover, the child can come to enjoy the excitements that belong to all these conflicts, provided they can be contained; and in the games, the children of a family introduce all the strains and stresses which belong to this kind of experimentation with disloyalties, even including the perceived tensions and jealousies that exist among the grown-up people in the environment. In a sense this is a good way of describing family life in theoretical terms. Perhaps the tremendous interest that children have in playing fathers and mothers derives from a gradual widening out of the experiencing of the experimentation with disloyalties.

Sometimes one can see how important these games are when a new child arrives rather late in the family and of course cannot make use of the brothers' and sisters' games because these have evolved a complexity which has a history for the older brothers and sisters. The new child may become involved in a mechanical way and feel severely eliminated or annihilated by the involvement, which is not a creative one, since the new child would need to start again and to build up from the simplest beginnings the complexity of cross-loyalties.

I know, of course, that there are positive and libidinal features in the feelings that belong to the family game, but the content making for excitement is very much associated with this matter of cross-loyalties. In this way the family game is the perfect preparation for life.

It will be seen that the school can easily provide tremendous relief for the child living in a family. For small children who play most of the time, the games played at school are not quite basic, and very soon they pass over into games which develop skills. Then there is the matter of the group discipline, and all this is a simplification very welcome for some, very irksome for others. Too early a simplification of the kind that school gives relative to the family game of children who live in a family must be looked at as an impoverishment, at any rate for those who can stand the family game, and whose families can stand up to the fact that the children are playing at families.

By contrast, it can be seen that the only or lonely child has everything to gain from going early to a play group, where, at any rate to some extent, the playing can have interpersonal relationships and cross-loyalties which are creative for the child.

These are the sort of reasons why there can never be a satisfactory decision from above in regard to the age at which children should go to school. In these delicate matters everything has to be examined afresh in every new case if good advice is to be given, and this means that in any one neighbourhood all kinds of provisions should be available. When in doubt, the child's home is the place where the richest experiences can be reached, but one has to be always on the look-out for the child who, for one reason or another, cannot be creative in imaginative play until he or she spends a few hours each day outside the family.

Primary school education belongs to the area in which the

child rather welcomes being distracted from working out the complexities that life offers by learning and by the adoption of specific loyalties and by acceptance of rules and standards along with the school uniform. Sometimes these conditions persist right through the adolescent period, but we are unhappy when the children allow such a thing to happen, however convenient it may be from the teachers' point of view. We expect in the adolescence of every boy and girl for there to reappear all the experimentation and cross-loyalties which appeared creatively in the family game, only this time the excitement comes not only from the fears roused, but also from the new and intense libidinal experiences which puberty has let loose.

The family is, of course, of tremendous value to the adolescent boy or girl, especially as each one of them is thoroughly frightened most of the time, even in health, since intense loving automatically produces intense hating. Where the family framework continues, the adolescent can act out fathers and mothers, which was the substance of the imaginative play at the 2–5-year stage of life at home.

It seems to me that the family is often thought of in terms of a structure maintained by the parents, in terms of a framework in which children can live and grow. It is thought of as a place where the children discover feelings of love and hate and where they can expect sympathy and tolerance as well as the exasperation which they engender. But what I have been saying has to do with my feeling that the part played by each child in the function of the family, in respect of the children's encounter with disloyalty, is somewhat understated. The family leads on to all manner of groupings, groupings that get wider and wider until they reach the size of the local society and society in general.

The reality of the world in which the children eventually must live as adults is one in which every loyalty involves something of an opposite nature which might be called a disloyalty, and the child who has had the chance to reach to all these things in the course of growth is in the best position to take a place in such a world.

Eventually, if one goes back, one can see that these disloyalties, as I am calling them, are an essential feature of living, and they stem from the fact that it is disloyal to everything that is not oneself if one is to be oneself. The most aggressive and therefore the most dangerous words in the languages of the world are to be found in the assertion I AM. It has to be admitted, however, that only those who have reached a stage at which they can make this assertion are really qualified as adult members of society.

Children Learning

*A paper read to a conference on Family
Evangelism under the auspices of the Christian
Teamwork Institute of Education, at Kingswood
College for Further Education, 5 June 1968*

I have come to speak at this conference as a human
being, a children's doctor, a child psychiatrist and a psychoanalyst. If I look back forty years I can see a change of
attitude. It is unlikely, forty years ago, that a psychoanalyst
could be expected by those engaged in religious teaching to
contribute positively. You know, I hope, that I have been
invited here not as a religious teacher, nor even as a Christian,
but as someone with a long experience in a limited field, one
who is intensely concerned with human problems of growth,
living and fulfilment. Your chairman said something about
my knowing more than anyone else about childhood behaviour. He got that off the back of some book! The contribution you would like me to make is that I know about
more than just the surface phenomena, or behaviour on top
of the whole personality structure. The word 'fulfilment'
comes in here. There is a class of people who study childhood
behaviour and miss out unconscious motivation and the relation of behaviour to conflict within the person, and so get
completely out of touch with anybody who is teaching about
religion – I think that that is what your chairman meant, that
I was interested in the developing human being in the family
and the social setting.

Brought up as a Wesleyan Methodist, I suppose I just

grew up out of church religious practice, and I am always glad that my religious upbringing was of a kind that allowed for growing up out of. I know that I am talking to an enlightened audience for whom religion does not mean just going to church every Sunday. May I say that it seems to me that what is commonly called religion arises out of human nature, whereas there are some who think of human nature as rescued from savagery by a revelation from outside human nature.

There are many matters of great significance we might discuss together once we have decided to look and see whether there could be a positive contribution from the psychoanalytic side to religious teaching and even to the practice of religion. Do you need miracles in this age of close, objective observation? Do you need to be addicted to the idea of an after-life? Do you need to put myth among the second-class citizens of thought? Do you need to go on robbing the individual child or adolescent or adult of his or her own innate goodness by inculcating morality?

I must keep to one subject in order to be contained within one hour and also within the limited area of my special experience. I think I may have been invited here today because of something I once said about a child's capacity to believe *in*. This leaves open the whole question of what you place at the end of the phrase. What I am doing is to separate out living experience from education. In education you can hand on to the child the beliefs that have meaning for yourself and that belong to the small cultural or religious area that you happen to be born into or to choose as an alternative to the one you were born into. But you will have success only in so far as the child has a capacity to believe in anything at all. The development of this capacity is not a matter of education, unless you extend the word to mean something that is not usually meant by it. It is a matter of the experience of the person as a developing baby and child in the matter of care. The mother comes into this, and perhaps the father and others who are in the immediate environment of the baby – but initially the mother.

You will see that for me there is always this matter of growth and development. I never think of the state of a person here and now except in relation to the environment and in relation to the growth of that individual from conception and certainly from the time around the birth date.

The individual baby is born with inherited tendencies that fiercely drive the individual on in a growth process. This includes the tendency towards integration of the personality, towards the wholeness of a personality in body and mind, and towards object-relating, which gradually becomes a matter of interpersonal relationships as the child begins to grow up and understand the existence of other people. All this comes from within the boy or girl. Nevertheless, these processes of growth cannot take place without a facilitating environment, especially at the start when a condition of dependence obtains which is near absolute. A facilitating environment must have a human quality, not a mechanical perfection, so the phrase 'good-enough mother' seems to me to meet the need for a description of what the child needs if the inherited growth processes are to become actual in the development of the individual child. In the beginning the whole of the development takes place because of the tremendously vital, inherited tendencies towards development – towards integration, towards growth, the thing that one day makes the child want to walk, and so on. If there is a good-enough environmental provision, these things take place in that child. But if the facilitating environment is not good enough, then the line of life is broken and the very powerful inherited tendencies cannot carry the child on to personal fulfilment.

A good-enough mother starts off with a high degree of adaptation to the baby's needs. That is what 'good-enough' means, this tremendous capacity that mothers ordinarily have to give themselves over to identification with the baby. Towards the end of a pregnancy and at the beginning of a child's life, they are so identified with the baby that they really practically know what the baby is feeling like, and so they can adapt themselves to the needs of the baby in such a way that the baby's needs are met. Then the baby is in the position of being able to make a developmental continuity of growth which is the beginning of health. The mother is laying down the basis for the mental health of the baby, and more than health – fulfilment and richness, with all the dangers and conflicts that these bring, with all the awkwardnesses that belong to growth and development.

So the mother, and the father too, though the father does not have the same physical relationship at the beginning, has this ability to identify with the baby without resentment, and to adapt to the baby's needs. The vast majority of babies in the world in the past several thousand years have had good-enough mothering at the beginning; otherwise the world would be more full of mad people than sane people, and it isn't. This identification of the woman with her baby presents a threat to some women; they wonder if they will ever get back their own individuality, and because of these anxieties some find it difficult to give themselves over to this extreme of adaptation at the beginning.

It is obvious that mother-figures meet the baby's instinctual needs. But that side of parent–infant relationship has been over-stressed in the first fifty years of psychoanalytic literature. It took a long time for the analytic world – and thought about child development has been powerfully influenced by the last sixty or so years of psychoanalytic thinking – to look, for example, at the importance of the way a baby is held; and yet, when you come to think of it, this is of primary significance. You could make a caricature of someone smoking a cigarette and holding the baby by the leg, swinging it round and putting it in the bath, and you know somehow that this is not what babies need. There are very subtle things here. I've watched and talked to thousands of mothers, and you see how they pick up the baby, supporting the head and the body. If you have got a child's body and head in your hands and do not think of that as a unity, and reach for a handkerchief or something, then the head has gone back and the child is in two pieces – head and body; the child screams and never forgets it. The awful thing is that nothing is ever forgotten. Then the child goes around with an absence of confidence in things. I think it is right to say that babies and little children do not remember when things went well, they remember when things went wrong, because they remember that suddenly the continuity of their life was snapped, and their neck went back or something, and it came through all the defences, and they reacted to it, and this is an extremely painful thing that has happened to them, something they cannot ever lose. And they have got to go round with it, and if that is in the pattern of their care, it builds up into a lack of confidence in the environment.

If things went well, they never say 'thank you', because they did not know it went well. In families there is this great area of unacknowledged debt which is no debt. There is nothing owing, but anybody who reaches stable adulthood could not have done it if somebody at the beginning had not taken him or her through the early stages.

This question of holding and handling brings up the whole issue of human reliability. The sort of thing I have been talking about could not be done by a computer – it must be *human* reliability (that is, unreliability, really). In the development of adaptation, the mother's great adaptation to the baby gradually becomes less; accordingly the baby begins to be frustrated and to be angry and needs to identify with the mother. I remember a baby of three months who, when feeding at the mother's breast, would put his hand to her mouth to feed her before he took her breast. He was able to get an idea of what the mother was feeling like.

The child can keep the idea of the mother or father or baby-sitter alive for so many minutes, but if the mother at that stage is away for two hours, then the *image* of the mother that the child has inside him wilts and begins to die. When the mother returns, she is another person. It is difficult to bring alive the *image* inside himself. For two years or so, the child does react very badly to separation from the mother. By two years old, the child actually knows the mother or father well enough to be able to be interested not just in an object or in a situation, but in an actual person. At two years the child needs to have the mother there if, for example, he goes into hospital. But always the baby needs the environmental stability that facilitates continuity of personal experience.

I learn a lot not only from talking to mothers and watching children, but also from treating grown people; they all become babies and children in the course of treatment. I have to pretend to be more grown-up than I am to deal with this. I have a patient at the moment; she is fifty-five years old and she can keep the *image* of me alive if she sees me three times a week. Twice a week is just possible. Once a week, although I give her a very long session, is not enough. The *image* wilts and the pain of seeing all the feelings and all the meaning going out is so great that she will say to me that it is not worth it, she would rather die. So the pattern of treatment has to depend on how the *image* of the parent-figure can be kept alive. One cannot help becoming a parent-figure whenever one is doing anything professionally reliable. You are nearly all, I expect, engaged in some sort of professionally reliable thing, and in that limited area you behave much better than you do at home, and your clients depend on you and get to lean on you.

Acts of human reliability make a communication long before speech means anything – the way the mother fits in when rocking the child, the sound and tone of her voice, all communicate long before speech is understood.

We are believing people. Here we are in this large hall and no one has been worried about the ceiling falling down. We have a belief in the architect. We are believing people because we are started off well by somebody. We received a silent communication over a period of time that we were loved in the sense that we could rely on the environmental provision and so get on with our growth and development.

A child who has not experienced preverbal care in terms of

holding and handling – human reliability – is a deprived
child. The only thing that can logically be applied to a
deprived child is love, love in terms of holding and handling.
To do it later in a child's life is difficult, but at any rate we
may try, as in the provision of residential care. The difficulty
comes from the child's need to make tests and to see if this
preverbal loving, holding, handling, and so on, stands up to
the destructiveness that comes with primitive loving. When
all goes well, this destructiveness becomes sublimated into
things like eating, kicking, playing, competition, and so on.
Nevertheless, the child is at this very primitive stage – here's
somebody to love, and then the next thing is destruction. If
you survive, then there is the *idea* of destruction instead. But
first of all there is destruction, and if you start to love a child
who was not loved in this preverbal sense, you may find
yourself in a mess; you find yourself being stolen from,
windows broken, the cat being tortured, and all sorts of
frightful things. And you have got to survive all this. You
will be loved because you have survived.

Why is it that if I stand up here and say that I had a good
start, it sounds like boasting? All I am in fact saying is that
nothing I am capable of is just me; it was either inherited, or
else somebody enabled me to get to the place where I am.
The reason it does sound like boasting is because it is impossible for me as a human being to believe that I did not
choose my own parents. So I am saying that I made a good
choice, aren't I clever? It seems silly, but we are dealing with
human nature, and in matters of human growth and development we need to be able to accept paradoxes; what we
feel and what can be observed to be true can be reconciled.
Paradoxes are not meant to be resolved; they are meant to be
observed. It is at this point that we begin to divide into two
camps. We must observe what it is that we feel, while at the
same time using our brains to work out what it is that we
have feelings about. Let's take my suggestion that the whole
of the preverbal expression of love in terms of holding and
handling has vital significance for each developing baby.

Then we can say that on the basis of what has been experienced by an individual, we may teach the concept of, say, everlasting arms. We may use that word 'God', we can make a specific link with the Christian church and doctrine, but it is a series of steps. Teaching comes into place there on the basis of what the individual child has the capacity to believe in. If in the case of moral teaching we take the line that we are going to treat certain things as sinful, how far are we sure that we are not robbing the growing child of the capacity *on his own* to come to a personal sense of right and wrong, to come to this out of his own development? One can often rob an individual of a terribly important moment when the feeling is: 'I have an impulse to do such and such, but I also . . .' and they come to some sort of personal developmental phase, which would have been completely broken across if somebody had said, 'You're not to do that, it's wrong.' Then they would either comply, in which case they have given up, or else they would defy, in which case nobody has gained anything, and there is no growth.

From my point of view, what you teach can only be implanted on what capacity is already present in the individual child, based on the early experiences and on the continuation of reliable holding in terms of the ever-widening circle of family and school and social life.

Adolescent Immaturity

A paper given to the 21st Annual Meeting of the British Student Health Association, held at Newcastle-upon-Tyne, 18 July 1968

Preliminary Observations

My approach to this vast subject must derive from the area of my especial experience. The remarks that I may make must be cast in the mould of the psychotherapeutic attitude. As a psychotherapist I naturally find myself thinking in terms of

the emotional development of the individual;

the role of the mother and of the parents;

the family as a natural development in terms of childhood needs;

the role of schools and other groupings seen as extensions of the family idea, and relief from set family patterns;

the special role of the family in its relation to the needs of adolescents;

the immaturity of the adolescent;

the gradual attainment of maturity in the life of the adolescent;

the individual's attainment of an identification with social groupings and with society, without too great a loss of personal spontaneity;

the structure of society, the word being used as a collective noun, society being composed of individual units, whether mature or immature;

the abstraction of politics and economics and philosophy and culture seen as the culmination of natural growing processes;

the world as a superimposition of a thousand million individual patterns, the one upon the other.

The dynamic is the growth process, this being inherited by each individual. Taken for granted here is the good-enough facilitating environment, which at the start of each individual's growth and development is a *sine qua non*. There are genes which determine patterns and an inherited tendency to grow and to achieve maturity, and yet nothing takes place in emotional growth except in relation to the environmental provision, which must be good enough. It will be noticed that the word 'perfect' does not enter into this statement – perfection belongs to machines, and the imperfections that are characteristic of human adaptation to need are an essential quality in the environment that facilitates.

Basic to all this is the idea of *individual dependence*, dependence being at first near-absolute and changing gradually and in an ordered way to relative dependence and towards independence. Independence does not become absolute, and the individual seen as an autonomous unit is, in fact, never independent of environment, though there are ways by which in maturity the individual may *feel* free and independent, as much as makes for happiness and for a sense of having a personal identity. By means of cross-identifications the sharp line between the me and the not-me is blurred.

All I have done so far is to enumerate various sections of an encyclopaedia of human society in terms of a perpetual ebullition on the surface of the cauldron of individual growth seen collectively and recognized as dynamic. The bit that I can deal with here is necessarily limited in size, and it is important therefore for me to place what I shall say against the vast back-screen of humanity, humanity that can be viewed in many different ways and that can be looked at with the eye at the one or the other end of the telescope.

Illness or Health?

As soon as I leave generalities and start to become specific, I must choose to include this and to reject that. For instance, there is the matter of personal psychiatric illness. Society includes all its individual members. The structure of society is built up and maintained by its members who are psychiatrically healthy. Nevertheless, it must needs contain those who are ill – for instance, society contains:

the immature (immature in age);

the psychopathic (end-product of deprivation – persons who, *when hopeful*, must make society acknowledge the fact of their deprivation, whether of a good or loved object or of a satisfactory *structure* that could be relied on to stand the strains that arise out of spontaneous movement);

the neurotic (bedevilled by unconscious motivation and ambivalence);

the moody (hovering between suicide and some alternative, which may include the highest achievements in terms of contribution);

the schizoid (who have a life-work already set out for them, namely the establishment of themselves, each one as an individual with a sense of identity and of feeling real);

the schizophrenic (who cannot, at least in ill phases, feel real, who may, at best, achieve something on a basis of living by proxy).

To these we must add the most awkward category – one that includes many persons who get themselves into positions of authority or responsibility – namely, the paranoid, those who are dominated by a system of thought. This system must be constantly shown to explain everything, the alternative (for the individual ill that way) being acute confusion of ideas, a sense of chaos, and a loss of all predictability.

In any description of psychiatric illness there is overlapping. People do not group themselves nicely into illness groupings. It is this that makes psychiatry so difficult for physicians and surgeons to understand. They say: 'You have the disease and we have (or will have in a year or two) the cure.' No psychiatric label exactly meets the case, and least of all the label 'normal' or 'healthy'.

We could look at society in terms of illness, and how its ill members, one way and another, compel attention, and how society becomes coloured by the illness groupings that start in the individuals; or, indeed, we could examine the way in which families and social units may produce individuals who are psychiatrically healthy except that the social unit that happens to be theirs at any one time distorts them or renders them ineffectual.

I have not chosen to look at society in this way. I have chosen to look at society *in terms of its healthiness*, that is, in its growth or perpetual rejuvenation naturally out of the health of its psychiatrically healthy members. I say this even though I do know that at times the proportion of psychiatrically unhealthy members in a group may be too high, so that the healthy elements, even in their aggregate of health, cannot carry them. Then the social unit becomes itself a psychiatric casualty.

I therefore intend to look at society as if it were composed of psychiatrically healthy persons. Even so, society will be found to have problems enough! Enough indeed!

It will be noted that I have not used the word 'normal'. This word is too well tied up with facile thinking. But I do believe that there is such a thing as psychiatric health, and this means that I feel justified in studying society (as others have done) in terms of its being the statement in collective terms of individual growth towards personal fulfilment. The axiom is that since there is no society except as a structure brought about and maintained and constantly reconstructed by individuals, there is no personal fulfilment without society, and no society apart from the collective growth processes of the individuals that compose it. And we must learn to cease looking for the world-citizen, and be contented to find here and there persons whose social unit extends beyond the local version of society, or beyond nationalism, or beyond the boundaries of a religious sect. In effect, we need to accept the fact that psychiatrically healthy persons depend for their health and for their personal fulfilment on *loyalty to a de-limited area of society*, perhaps the local bowls club. And why not? It is only if we look for Gilbert Murray everywhere that we come to grief.

The Main Thesis

A positive statement of my thesis brings me immediately to the tremendous changes that have taken place in the last fifty years in regard to the importance of good-enough mothering. This includes fathers, but fathers must allow me to use the term 'maternal' to describe the total attitude to babies and their care. The term 'paternal' must necessarily come a little later than maternal. Gradually the father as male becomes a significant factor. And then follows the family, the basis of which is the union of fathers and mothers, in a sharing of responsibility for this that they have done together, that which we call a new human being – a baby.

Let me refer to the maternal provision. We now know that it does matter how a baby is held and handled, that it matters who it is that is caring for the baby, and whether this is in fact the mother, or someone else. In our theory of child care, continuity of care has become a central feature of the concept of the facilitating environment, and we see that by this continuity of environmental provision, and only by this, the new baby in dependence may have a continuity in the line of his or her life, not a pattern of reacting to the unpredictable and for ever starting again.[1]

I can refer here to Bowlby's work: the two-year-old child's reaction to loss of mother's person (even temporary), if

1. 'Joanna Field' (M. Milner), *A Life of One's Own*, London, Chatto & Windus, 1934; Harmondsworth, Penguin Books, 1952.

beyond the time-stretch of the baby's capacity to keep alive her image, has found general acceptance, though it has yet to be fully exploited;[2] but the idea behind this extends to the whole subject of continuity of care and dates from the beginning of the baby's personal life, that is, before the baby objectively perceives the whole mother as the person she is.

Another new feature: as child psychiatrists, we are not just concerned with health. I wish this were true of psychiatry in general. We are concerned with the richness of the happiness that builds up in health and *does not build up* in psychiatric ill health, even when the genes could take the child towards fulfilment.

We now look at slums and poverty not only with horror, but also with an eye open to the possibility that for a baby or a small child a slum family may be more secure and 'good' as a facilitating environment than a family in a lovely house where there is an absence of the common persecutions.[3] Also, we can feel it is worthwhile to consider the essential differences that exist between social groups in terms of accepted customs. Take swaddling, as opposed to the infant's permission to explore and to kick that obtains almost universally in society as we know it in Britain. What is the local attitude to pacifiers, to thumb-sucking, to auto-erotic exercises in general? How do people react to the natural incontinences of early life and their relation to continence? And so on. The phase of Truby King is still in the process of being lived down by adults trying to give their babies the right to discover a personal morality, and we can see this in a reaction to indoctrination that goes to the extreme of extreme permissiveness. It might turn out that the differences between the white citizen of the United States and the black-skinned citizen of that country is not so much a matter of skin colour

2. John Bowlby, *Attachment and Loss*, London, Hogarth Press and the Institute of Psycho-Analysis, 1969; New York, Basic Books, 1969; Harmondsworth, Penguin Books, 1971.

3. Overcrowding, starvation, infestation, the constant threat from physical disease and disaster and from the laws promulgated by a benevolent society.

as of breast-feeding. Incalculable is the envy of the white bottle-fed population of the black people, who are mostly, I believe, breast-fed.

It may be noticed that I am concerned with unconscious motivation, something that is not altogether a popular concept. The data I need are not to be culled from a form-filling questionnaire. A computer cannot be programmed to give motives that are unconscious in the individuals who are the guinea pigs of an investigation. This is where those who have spent their lives doing psychoanalysis must scream out for sanity against the insane belief in surface phenomena that characterizes computerized investigations of human beings.

More Confusion   Another source of confusion is the glib assumption that if mothers and fathers bring up their babies and children well, there will be less trouble. Far from it! This is very germane to my main theme, because I wish to imply that when we look at adolescence, where the successes and failures of baby and child care come home to roost, some of the present-day troubles belong to the positive elements in modern upbringing and in modern attitudes to the rights of the individual.

If you do all you can to promote personal growth in your offspring, you will need to be able to deal with startling results. If your children find themselves at all, they will not be contented to find anything but the whole of themselves, and that will include the aggression and destructive elements in themselves as well as the elements that can be labelled loving. There will be this long tussle which you will need to survive.

With some of your children you will be lucky if your ministrations quickly enable them to use symbols, to play, to dream, to be creative in satisfying ways, but even so the road to this point may be rocky. And in any case you will make mistakes and these mistakes will be seen and felt to be disastrous, and your children will try to make you feel responsible for setbacks even when you are not in fact responsible. Your children simply say: 'I never asked to be born.'

Your rewards come in the richness that may gradually appear in the personal potential of this or that boy or girl. And if you succeed, you must be prepared to be jealous of your children, who are getting better opportunities for personal development than you had yourselves. You will feel rewarded if one day your daughter asks you to do some baby-sitting for her, indicating thereby that she thinks you may be able to do this satisfactorily; or if your son wants to be like you in some way, or falls in love with a girl you would have liked yourself, had you been younger. Rewards come *indirectly*. And of course you know you will not be thanked.

Death and Murder in the Adolescent Process

I now jump to the re-enactment of these matters as they affect the task of parents when their children are at puberty, or in the throes of adolescence.

Although a great deal is being published concerning the individual and social problems that appear in this decade, wherever adolescents are free to express themselves, there may be room for a further personal comment on the content of adolescent fantasy.

In the time of adolescent growth, boys and girls awkwardly and erratically emerge out of childhood and away from dependence, and grope towards adult status. Growth is not just a matter of inherited tendency; it is also a matter of a highly complex interweaving with the facilitating environment. If the family is still there to be used, it is used in a big way; and if the family is no longer there to be used, or to be set aside (negative use), then small social units need to be provided to contain the adolescent growth process. The same problems loom at puberty that were present in the early stages when these same children were relatively harmless toddlers or infants. It is worth noting that if you have done well at the early stages and are still doing well, you cannot count on a smooth running of the machine. In fact, you can expect troubles. Certain troubles are inherent at these later stages.

It is valuable to compare adolescent ideas with those of childhood. If, in the fantasy of early growth, there is contained *death*, then at adolescence there is contained *murder*. Even when growth at the period of puberty goes ahead without major crises, one may need to deal with acute problems of management, because growing up means taking the parent's place. *It really does*. In the unconscious fantasy, growing up is inherently an aggressive act. And the child is now no longer child-size.

It is legitimate, I believe, as well as useful, to look at the game 'I'm the King of the Castle'. This game belongs to the male element in boys and girls. (The theme could also be stated in terms of the female element in girls and boys, but I cannot do this here.) This is a game of early latency, and at puberty it becomes changed into a life-situation.

'I'm the King of the Castle' is a statement of personal being. It is an achievement of individual emotional growth. It is a position that implies the death of all rivals or the establishment of dominance. The expected attack is shown in the next words: 'And you're the dirty rascal' (or 'Get down, you dirty rascal'). Name your rival and you know where you are. Soon the dirty rascal knocks the King over and in turn becomes King. The Opies (1951) refer to this rhyme. They say that the game is exceedingly old, and that Horace (20 BC) gives the children's words as:

> *Rex erit qui recte faciet;*
> *Qui non faciet, non erit.*[4]

We need not think that human nature has altered. What we need to do is to look for the everlasting in the ephemeral. We need to translate this childhood game into the language of the unconscious motivation of adolescence and society. If the child is to become adult, then this move is achieved over

4. From *The Oxford Dictionary of Nursery Rhymes*, edited by Iona and Peter Opie, Oxford University Press, 1951.

the dead body of an adult. (I must take it for granted that the reader knows that I am referring to unconscious fantasy, the material that underlies playing.) I know, of course, that boys and girls may manage to go through this stage of growth in a continued setting of accord with actual parents, and without necessarily manifesting rebellion at home. But it is wise to remember that rebellion belongs to the freedom you have given your child by bringing him or her up in such a way that he or she exists in his or her own right. In some instances it could be said: 'You sowed a baby and you reaped a bomb.' In fact, this is always true, but it does not always look like it.

In the total unconscious fantasy belonging to growth at puberty and in adolescence, there is *the death of someone*. A great deal can be managed in play and by displacements, and on the basis of cross-identifications; but, in the psychotherapy of the individual adolescent (and I speak as a psychotherapist), there is to be found death and personal triumph as something inherent in the process of maturation and in the acquisition of adult status. This makes it difficult enough for parents and guardians. Be sure it makes it difficult also for the individual adolescents themselves, who come with shyness to the murder and the triumph that belong to maturation at this crucial stage. The unconscious theme may become manifest as the experience of a suicidal impulse, or as actual suicide. Parents can help only a little; the best they can do is to *survive*, to survive intact, and without changing colour, without relinquishment of any important principle. This is not to say they may not themselves grow.

A proportion at adolescence will become casualties or will attain to a kind of maturity in terms of sex and marriage, perhaps becoming parents like the parents themselves. This may do. But somewhere in the background is a life-and-death struggle. The situation lacks its full richness if there is a too easy and successful avoidance of the clash of arms.

This brings me to my main point, the difficult one of the *immaturity* of the adolescent. Mature adults must know about this and must believe in their own maturity as never before or after.

It will be appreciated that it is difficult to state this without being misunderstood, since it so easily sounds like a downgrading to talk of immaturity. But this is not intended.

A child of any age (say, six years) may suddenly need to become responsible, perhaps because of the death of a parent or because of the break-up of a family. Such a child must be prematurely old and must lose spontaneity and play and carefree creative impulse. More frequently, an adolescent may be in this position, suddenly finding himself or herself with the vote or with the responsibility for running a college. Of course, if circumstances alter (if, for instance, you become ill or die, or you are in financial straits), then you cannot avoid inviting the boy or girl to become a responsible agent before the time is ripe; perhaps younger children have to be cared for or educated, and there may be an absolute need for money to live. However, it is different when, as a matter of deliberate policy, the adults hand over responsibility; indeed, to do this can be a kind of letting your children down at a critical moment. In terms of the game, or the life-game, you abdicate just as they come to killing you. Is anyone happy? Certainly not the adolescent, who now becomes the establishment. Lost is all the imaginative activity and striving of immaturity. Rebellion no longer makes sense, and the adolescent who wins too early is caught in his own trap, must turn dictator, and must stand up waiting to be killed – to be killed not by a new generation of his own children, but by siblings. Naturally, he seeks to control them.

Here is one of the many places where society ignores unconscious motivation at its peril. Surely the everyday material of the psychotherapist's work could be used a little by sociologists and by politicians, as well as by ordinary people who are adults – that is to say, adult in their own limited spheres of influence, even if not always in their private lives.

What I am stating (dogmatically, in order to be brief) is that the adolescent is *immature*. Immaturity is an essential element of health at adolescence. There is only one cure for immaturity and that is the *passage of time* and the growth into maturity that time may bring. These together do, in the end, result in the emergence of an adult person. This process cannot be hurried or slowed up, though indeed it can be broken into and destroyed, or it can wither up from within in psychiatric illness.

I think of a girl who kept me in touch with herself throughout her adolescence. She was not under treatment. At fourteen she was suicidal. Poems marked all the stages she was going through. Here's one, when she was just beginning to emerge, very short:

> If once you're hurt – withdraw your hand
> Vow not to speak those words;
> And then beware – or loving unaware
> You'll find your hand outstretched again.

So she is just coming through from the suicidal phase to the one where there's a little bit of hope sometimes. Now, at twenty-three, this same young woman has founded her own home, has found the beginnings of a place in society, and has become able to depend on her partner. She not only enjoys her home and her child, but also has been able to encompass such sorrow as has come her way and to find a new way of looking at coming to terms with her parents, without losing her personal identity. The passage of time has done this.

I think of a boy who could not adjust to the restrictions of a rather good school. He ran away to sea and thereby avoided being expelled. For some years he put a severe strain on his mother, but she took responsibility for him. After a while, he came back and worked himself into a university where he did well, because by that time he could talk languages that nobody else had heard of. Then he took various jobs until he settled down to a career. I believe he is married, but I do not wish to give the impression that marriage is the total solution – though marriage does often mark the beginning of a socialization. These stories are both ordinary, and extraordinary.

Immaturity is a precious part of the adolescent scene. In this is contained the most exciting features of creative thought, new and fresh feeling, ideas for new living. Society needs to be shaken by the aspirations of those who are not responsible. If the adults abdicate, the adolescent becomes prematurely, and by false process, adult. Advice to society could be: for the sake of adolescents, and of their immaturity, do not allow them to step up and attain a false maturity by handing over to them responsibility that is not yet theirs, even though they may fight for it.

With the proviso that the adult does not abdicate, we may surely think of the strivings of adolescents to find themselves and to determine their own destiny as the most exciting thing that we can see in life around us. The adolescent's idea of an ideal society is exciting and stimulating, but the point about adolescence is its immaturity and the fact of not being responsible. This, its most sacred element, lasts only a few years, and it is a property that must be lost to each individual as maturity is reached.

I constantly remind myself that it is the state of adolescence that society perpetually carries, not the adolescent boy or girl who, alas, in a few years becomes an adult, and becomes only too soon identified with some kind of frame in which new babies, new children and new adolescents may be free to have vision and dreams and new plans for the world.

Triumph belongs to this attainment of maturity by growth process. Triumph does not belong to the false maturity based on a facile impersonation of an adult. Terrible facts are locked up in this statement.

Nature of Immaturity

It is necessary to look for a moment into the nature of immaturity. We must not expect the adolescent to be aware of his or her immaturity, or to know what the features of immaturity are. Nor do we need to understand at all. What counts is that the adolescents' challenge be met. Met by whom?

I confess that I feel I am insulting this subject by talking about it. The more easily we verbalize, the less are we effectual. Imagine someone talking down to adolescents and saying to them: 'The exciting part of you is your immaturity!' This would be a gross example of failure to meet the adolescent challenge. Perhaps this phrase 'a meeting of the challenge' represents a return to sanity, because *understanding* has become replaced by *confrontation*. The word 'confrontation' is used here to mean that a grown-up person stands up and claims the right to have a personal point of view, one that may have the backing of other grown-up people.

Potential at Adolescence Let us look and see what sorts of things adolescents have not reached.

The changes of puberty take place at varying ages, even in healthy children. Boys and girls can do nothing but wait for these changes. This waiting around puts a considerable strain on all, but especially on the late developers; so the late ones can be found imitating those who have developed early, and this leads to false maturities based on identifications rather than on the innate growth process. In any case, the sexual change is not the only one. There is a change towards physical growth and the acquisition of real strength; therefore, real danger arrives which gives violence a new meaning. Along with strength come cunning and know-how.

Only with the passage of time and the experience of living can a boy or girl gradually accept responsibility for all that is happening in the world of personal fantasy. Meanwhile there is a strong liability for aggression to become manifest in suicidal form; alternatively, aggression turns up in the form of a search for persecution, which is an attempt to get out of the madness of a persecutory delusional system. Where persecution is delusionally expected, there is a liability for it to be provoked in an attempt to get away from madness and delusion. One psychiatrically ill boy (or girl) with a well-formed delusional system can spark off a group system of thought and lead to episodes based on *provoked* persecution.

Logic holds no sway once the delicious simplification of a persecutory position has been achieved.

But most difficult of all is the strain felt in the individual belonging to the *unconscious* fantasy of *sex* and the rivalry that is associated with sexual object-choice.

The adolescent, or the boy and girl who are still in the process of growing, cannot yet take responsibility for the cruelty and the suffering, for the killing and the being killed, that the world scene offers. This saves the individual at this stage from the extreme reaction against personal latent aggression, namely, suicide (a pathological acceptance of responsibility for all the evil that is, or that can be thought of). It seems that the latent sense of guilt of the adolescent is terrific, and it takes years for the development in an individual of a capacity to discover in the self the balance of the good and the bad, the hate and the destruction that go with love, within the self. In this sense, maturity belongs to later life, and the adolescent cannot be expected to see beyond the next stage, which belongs to the early twenties.

It is sometimes taken for granted that boys and girls who 'hop in and out of bed', as the saying goes, and who achieve intercourse (and perhaps a pregnancy or two), have reached sexual maturity. But they themselves know that this is not true, and they begin to despise sex as such. It's too easy. Sexual maturity needs to include all the unconscious fantasy of sex, and the individual needs ultimately to be able to reach to an acceptance of all that turns up in the mind along with object-choice, object-constancy, sexual satisfaction and sexual interweaving. Also, there is the sense of guilt that is appropriate in terms of the total unconscious fantasy.

Construction, Reparation, Restitution The adolescent cannot yet know what satisfaction there can be attained from participation in a project that needs to include within itself the quality of dependability. It is not possible for the adolescent to know how much the job, because of its social contribution, lessens the personal sense of guilt (that belongs to unconscious aggressive drives, closely linked with object-relating and with love) and so helps to lessen the fear within, and the degree of suicidal impulse or accident-proneness.

Idealism   One of the exciting things about adolescent boys and girls can be said to be their idealism. They have not yet settled down into disillusionment, and the corollary of this is that they are free to formulate ideal plans. Art students, for instance, can see that art could be taught well, so they clamour for art to be taught well. Why not? What they do not take into account is the fact that there are only a few people who can teach art well. Or students see that physical conditions are cramped and could be improved, so they scream. It is for others to find the money. 'Well,' they say, 'just abandon the defence programme and spend the cash on new university buildings!' It is not for the adolescent to take a long-term view, which may come more naturally to those who have lived through many decades and begun to grow old.

All of this is absurdly condensed. It omits the prime significance of friendship. It omits a statement of the position of those who make a life without marriage or with marriage postponed. And it leaves out the vital problem of bisexuality, which becomes resolved but never entirely resolved in terms of heterosexual object-choice and of object-constancy. Also, a great deal has been taken for granted that has to do with the theory of creative playing. Moreover, there is the cultural heritage; it cannot be expected that, at the age of adolescence, the average boy or girl has more than an inkling of man's cultural heritage, for one must work hard at this even to know about it. At sixty years old, these who are boys and girls now will be breathlessly making up for lost time in the pursuit of riches that belong to civilization and its accumulated by-products.

The main thing is that adolescence is more than physical puberty, though largely based on it. Adolescence implies growth, and this growth takes time. And, while growing is in progress, *responsibility must be taken by parent-figures*. If parent-figures abdicate, then the adolescents must make a jump to a false maturity and lose their greatest asset: freedom to have ideas and to act on impulse.

Summary

In brief, it is exciting that adolescence has become vocal and active, but the adolescent striving that makes itself felt over the whole world today needs to be met, needs to be given reality by an act of confrontation. Confrontation must be personal. Adults are needed if adolescents are to have life and liveliness. Confrontation belongs to containment that is non-retaliatory, without vindictiveness, but having its own strength. It is salutary to remember that the present student unrest and its manifest expression may be in part a product of the attitude we are proud to have attained towards baby care and child care. Let the young alter society and teach grown-ups how to see the world afresh; but, where there is the challenge of the growing boy or girl, there let an adult meet the challenge. And it will not necessarily be nice.

In the unconscious fantasy these are matters of life and death.

Part 3

Reflections on Society

Thinking and the Unconscious

An article contributed to the Liberal Magazine,
March 1945

The Liberal Party is linked in my mind with the use
of brains and the attempt to think things out, and it is surely
for this reason that it tends to appeal to those whose work
involves an acquaintance with pure science. Scientists
naturally wish to carry over into their politics something
from their own discipline. In human affairs, however,
thinking is but a snare and a delusion unless the unconscious
is taken into account. I refer to both meanings of the word,
'unconscious' meaning deep and not readily available, and
also meaning repressed, or actively kept from availability
because of the pain that belongs to its acceptance as part of
the self.

Unconscious feelings sway bodies of people at critical
moments, and who is to say that this is bad or good? It is just
a fact, and one that has to be taken into account all the
time by rational politicians if nasty shocks are to be
avoided. In fact, thinking men and women can only be
safely turned loose in the field of planning if they have qualified in this matter of the true understanding of unconscious
feelings.

Politicians are used to digging down into the depths intui-
tively, like artists of all kinds, discovering and bringing to
light the wonderful and awful phenomena that belong to
human nature. But the intuitive method has its drawbacks,
one of the greatest of which is that intuitive people are liable

to be hopeless at talking about the things they 'know' so easily. I think we would always rather hear the thinkers talking about what they are thinking out than hear the intuitive people talking about what they know. But when it comes to having our lives planned for us, heaven help us if the thinkers take over. Firstly, they but seldom believe in the importance of the unconscious at all; and, secondly, even if they do, man's understanding of human nature is not yet so complete as to enable thinking things out entirely to replace feeling. The danger is partly that the thinkers make plans that look marvellous. Each flaw as it appears is dealt with by a still more brilliant piece of thinking out, and in the end the masterpiece of rational construction is overthrown by a little detail like GREED that has been left out of account – the nett result being a new victory for unreason, with its consequence: an increase in the public distrust of logic.

In my own personal view the subject of economics, as it has grown up and been presented to us in England in the past twenty years, is an example of just such a matter for sadness. For clear thinking in regard to an almost infinitely complex matter, economists are unrivalled. And the thinking was needed. Nevertheless, to one whose job keeps him all the time in touch with the unconscious, economics has often seemed like a science of Greed in which all mention of Greed is banned. I put Greed with a capital letter, because I mean something more than greediness, the thing children get slapped for; I mean Greed, the primitive love impulse, the thing we are all frightened to own up to, but which is basic in our natures, and which we cannot do without, unless we give up our claim to physical and mental health. I would suggest that healthy economics acknowledges the existence and value (as well as the danger) of personal and collective Greed, and tries to harness it. Unsound economics, on the other hand, pretends that Greed is only to be found in certain pathological individuals or gangs of such individuals, and assumes that these individuals can be exterminated or locked up, and builds on that assumption. The assumption being a false one, a great deal of clever economics is only clever; that is to say, it is great fun to read, but it is dangerous as a foundation for planning.

The unconscious may be an awful nuisance to the thinkers-out, but so is love to the bishops.

The Price of Disregarding
Psychoanalytic Research

A talk given to the National Association for Mental Health Annual Conference entitled 'The Price of Mental Health', at the Assembly Hall, Church House, Westminster, 25 February 1965

To assess the price we pay for neglecting psychoanalytic research findings, we must first inquire into the nature of psychoanalytic research. Is it just here that science splits itself into research that is acceptable and research that concerns itself with the unconscious? A major consideration must be that the public generally must not be expected to be interested in unconscious motivation.

It can be said that there are two roads to the truth: the poetic and the scientific. Research findings relate to the scientific approach. Scientific research, which may be imaginative and creative work, is harnessed to the limited objective and to the result of experiment, and to prediction.

The link between poetic truth and scientific truth is surely in the person, in you and me. The poet in me reaches to a whole truth in a flash, and the scientist in me gropes towards a facet of the truth; as the scientist reaches the immediate objective, a new objective presents itself.

Poetic truth has certain advantages. For the individual, poetic truth offers deep satisfactions, and in the new expression of an old truth there is opportunity for new creative experience in terms of beauty. It is very difficult, however, to use poetic truth. Poetic truth is a matter of feeling, and we may not all feel the same about one problem. By scientific truth, with limited objective, we hope to bring people who can use their minds and who can be influenced by intellectual considerations to agreement in certain areas of practice. In poetry, something true crystallizes out; to plan our lives we need science. But science boggles at the problem of human nature, and tends to lose sight of the whole human being.

I was thinking of this when watching the T V presentation of Sir Winston Churchill's state funeral. What exhausted me as I sat at ease was the weight of the coffin and the tremendous strain borne for us all by those eight bearers. The burden of the ceremony rested on the shoulders of these men, who have now been suitably decorated. We were told inside stories of the near-collapse of one or other bearer, and it went round that the lead-lined coffin weighed half a ton, later reduced to five hundredweight.

Now, I knew a man of invention, an applied scientist, who had an idea. He invented and tried to put on the market a coffin that was very light. Had this man consulted a dozen psychoanalysts, he would have found general agreement among them that the bearers' burden is the burden of unconscious guilt, a symbol of grief. A light coffin would imply a denial of grief, a flippancy.

It is true that any feeling person could have poetically reacted to this. But now consider a planning commission, with high-grade civil servants thinking things out for another state funeral. In the area of top-grade intellectual process, an alternative to poetic truth has to be found, and this is called scientific inquiry. Science would be invoked and the first scientific experiment would concern itself with the blood pressure changes in men who shoulder heavy burdens. A hundred research projects leap to the mind. But (and this is the question), added up, would these projects take us to the concept of unconscious symbolism and to grief? This is where psychoanalysis takes us. I must ask: how could psychoanalytic research be used? What investigation could be called psychoanalytic research?

(I think I must ignore all that psychoanalysts have written for each other.)

Psychoanalytic research is not to be cramped into the pattern that suits research in the physical sciences. Every analyst is doing research, but the research is not planned as such because the analyst must follow the changing needs and the maturing objectives of the person undergoing analysis. This fact can never be circumvented. The treatment of the patient cannot be warped by research needs, and no setting for an observation can ever be repeated. The best is that the analyst looks back at what has happened and relates this to theory, and modifies theory accordingly.

No doubt a research project could be planned; I give a plan now: a suitable research worker, with a working knowledge of the theory of human growth, could make a formal visit to ten analysts, armed with a fee and a single simple question. I give a very simple specific example. The question might well be: how has the idea of BLACK come into the material of the analyses that you have been conducting during the past month?

On this material a valuable paper could be written, and it would include the idea of black as it appeared in patients' dreams and in children's playing, and it would reveal something of the unconscious symbolism that the idea carries, and the unconscious reactions of various types of individuals to black. The second question would be: do your observations support current psychoanalytic theory or do they call for modification of that theory? One result would be the discovery that there is much that is not yet known about the meaning of black in the unconscious. But a great deal is known, and is waiting to be harvested.

What is the price of ignoring this piece of research that could so easily be done? One price is a serious one in terms of continuing misunderstanding on the part of white-skinned people in relation to black, and of the dark millions in relation to whites. What is the price of our systematically wasting the systematic observing that is being done by every practising analyst who is awake while working?

It will have been observed that psychoanalytic research

has but little to do with rats and dogs, or with extended parlour games or with statistical assessment. The material for psychoanalytic research is essentially the human being . . . being, feeling, acting, relating and contemplating.

For me, analytic research is the collective experience of analysts. This simply needs to be assembled intelligently. We have each one of us done a tremendous quantity of detailed observation and we are bursting at the seams with understanding that is being wasted. But our work does concern itself with unconscious motivation, and this cuts us off from planners. In order to find a public to read his findings, the scientist (in human affairs), alas, must ignore the unconscious.

Perhaps we must just accept the fact that unconscious motivation is not society's cup of tea, except when it crystallizes out in some art form. Accepting this, we may look at the question again: what price do we pay . . .? And answer that we pay the price of just staying as we are, playthings of economics and of politics and of fate. Personally, I do not complain.

What follows is no more than an enumeration of costly examples of society's negative reaction to the union of the concept of the unconscious to scientific inquiry, and I give these without any idea that any use can be made of them. I do not have to prove here that psychoanalysis is the best treatment. Psychoanalysis certainly does provide a unique form of education for the analyst, and does so even when a case fails as a therapeutic procedure. If I am right in the simple theme that I am offering in this paper, then a training in psychoanalysis and the practice of psychoanalysis should be rated highly when a man or woman wishes to become educated to deal with human beings, healthy or sick.

Let me assume that instead of asking about 'black', the research workers were to enquire about war, the bomb and the population explosion.

War. Discussion of the unconscious value of war to the individual or to groups is practically taboo. Yet if this is left out of account, the price that will certainly be paid is no less than the disaster of a third world war.

The bomb. The unconscious symbolism of thermonuclear physics and of its application in terms of bombs could be examined. It is the analysts who concern themselves with borderline cases (schizoid personalities) who have information in this field. I am thinking of the bomb as an example in physics of personality disintegration in dynamic psychology.

Population explosion. Population explosion is usually studied in terms of economics, but there is more to be said and the subject is not covered by the term 'sexuality'. Certainly the difficulties in control of over-population come into the field of everyday psychoanalytic practice. But, as I have already said, the psychoanalyst has to learn to contain what he learns, to resign himself to the fact that no one wants to know what a close and personal examination of human feelings reveals.

Let me look for a moment into the vast territory of the psychiatrist, although I am not, strictly speaking, a psychiatrist.

Adult Psychiatry

In certain hospitals and clinics for adult mental patients the psychiatrists have added to their modern humane attitude an attempt to apply psychoanalytic findings. Other hospitals and clinics are contented with the humane attitude, difficult enough in itself when hundreds and even thousands of patients are crowded into one institution.

There is a considerable contribution to the understanding of depressive phenomena waiting to be lifted over from the psychoanalytic to the general psychiatric field. One thing in this respect (I choose one detail only) could be the need depressed persons have to be allowed to be depressed, to be kept alive and nursed over a period of time during which they may resolve their own inner conflicts, with or without psychotherapy.

One sometimes longs for the old word 'asylum', if that could mean a haven of rest for certain types of depressive patients who need to go into retreat. The price here has to be measured in terms of human waste and suffering. A practical detail is that the public shall accept suicide as a sad event, and not regard it as something indicating neglect on the part of the psychiatrist. The suicide threat provides a kind of blackmail which makes the young psychiatrist over-treat and over-protect his depressed patients, and this interferes with his human and humane management of the common depressive case.

A much more controversial subject, as you can see by listening to the biological side today, is that of research into schizophrenia, especially as schizophrenia is thought by many to be a disease, a result of inheritance and of biochemical disfunction. Research along these lines gets full support. But there is also a contribution to be got from psychoanalysis. Psychoanalysts have been forced, because of mistakes in diagnosis, to study schizoid persons, and they begin to have things to say about persons who bring schizoid symptomatology to the analyst for him to cope with. In this work of the psychoanalyst, schizophrenia appears as a disorder of the structuring of the personality.

The psychoanalyst is lucky who has a psychiatrist friend who will admit and care for one of his analytic patients who is in a phase of breakdown, a psychiatrist who will invite the analyst to continue to be in charge of the treatment, that is to say, the psychotherapeutic aspect of the treatment. Much psychoanalytic research is held up because of mutual suspicion between psychiatrist and psychoanalyst. The value of interdisciplinary activity in this field is not to be measured in terms of cure so much as in terms of the education of the psychoanalyst and of the psychiatrist.

On the whole, the trend in psychoanalysis is to see schizophrenia aetiologically as containing a reversal of the maturational processes of earliest infancy at the age at which absolute dependence is a fact. This would bring schizophrenia into the realm of the universal human struggle and would take it out of the realm of specific disease process. The medical world urgently needs this bit of sanity in so far as it is true, because disorders arising out of the human struggle should not be housed along with disorders secondary to degenerative processes.

I cannot bring myself to refer to my own subject, child psychiatry, because in making a condensed statement only a book would satisfy me.

Medical Practice

There is so vast an area of interaction between the field of medical practice and that of psychoanalysis that I cannot do more than refer to it. Integration is needed between doctors and psychoanalysts as also between the two aspects of the patient's split personality where psychosomatic disorder hides mental disorder. How can the psychosomatic patient achieve integration if those who are in charge of the case are at variance?

In all these fields, there are now professional organizations attempting to bridge the gaps and to integrate the findings of the various groups of research workers, including psychoanalysts, who always awkwardly peddle unconscious motivation.

Education

In the field of education the price of failure to use psychoanalytic research findings could be measured in terms of the neglect of the nursery school, primary education, all that has come from Margaret McMillan, Susan Isaacs and others. It could be measured in terms of a loss of the opportunity for creative learning, as opposed to being taught, or in terms of the interference with education of normal children by lack of facilities for the separation off from them of emotionally disturbed children, especially those with a failing environment at home.

To take a specific detail: corporal punishment at Eton or at any school which is designed for normal children with intact homes simply cannot be discussed in the same breath with the idea of corporal punishment in schools for deprived or antisocial boys and girls. Yet letters to *The Times* tend to ignore this fact. But the idea of corporal punishment has a differing unconscious significance for children according to whether they come into the category of healthy or ill. Teachers need to be introduced to the dynamics of infant and child care as much as they need to be taught what to teach, and they need to receive instruction in educational diagnosis.

Infant–Mother Relationship

I will not do more than briefly refer to the field of the infant-mother and the child–parent relationship, because I have already written my share of the psychoanalytic contribution to this subject. I will remind you, however, that psychoanalysis tends to show that the basis of mental health is not only hereditary, and is not only a matter of chance events; the basis of mental health is being actively laid down in the course of every infancy when the mother is good enough at her job, and in the span of every childhood that is being lived in a functioning family.

Psychoanalytic research gives maximal support, therefore, for the good-enough mother in her natural good-enough handling of her infant, to parental cooperation when it is in existence and continues to function satisfactorily, and to the family as a going concern, especially in the two developmental nodes: that of the toddler age and that of adolescence. Also, it gives the same support to the live teacher–parent interaction which characterizes the best of latency-period schooling.

Adolescence

Psychoanalytic research has contributed to a general theory of adolescence and its relation to puberty, joining its findings up with the work done by others on this developmental phase. Perhaps the present worldwide fact of adolescent boys and girls being adolescent during adolescence is itself (at least in part) a positive result of principles that stem from psychoanalytical research. I personally think so.

Those who value the family and who can think that the individual needs a family setting can find stronger support in psychoanalytic research than anywhere else. Psychoanalysis has shown the way in which the maturational process in individual growth needs a facilitating environment and how this facilitating environment is itself a highly complex thing, with its own developmental characteristics.

The Family Doctor

It is tempting to be topical and to add a word in general about the task of the family doctor. An inquiry among psychoanalysts at the time of the institution of the Health Service would have brought out knowledge already available then as to the unlimited hypochondria that is potential in the community, with its corresponding hypochondriacal anxiety in the doctor that underlies over-prescribing. It would not be reasonable, however, to expect this sort of information to be asked for at a time of planning, since planning has its own unconscious motivation. The price here has been heavy.

Further, information was ready, for the gathering in, that the public hates doctors and envies them, while each member of the public loves and trusts his or her own doctor; or the other way round, the public idealizes the medical profession, but, at the same time the individual members cannot find just the right doctor for themselves. Public and individual feelings tend to be opposed in respect of doctors. And the doctors are caught up in the same conflict of unconscious motivation. And the best of them are too much involved clinically to stand back and look at their problems objectively.

Special Case of Antisocial Tendency

Perhaps the most positive use made by society of psychoanalytic findings has been in the approach to the problem of antisocial behaviour. One reason for this may be that examination of the antisocial child leads to a history of deprivation, and to the child's reaction to a trauma of a special kind. In this way there is less resistance to research into the dynamics of the antisocial tendency, because what is found is not exactly unconscious motivation. Under suitable circumstances, the actual experience of deprivation in a child may often be recoverable, without resort to the analytic process. Society has made very good use of Bowlby's and the Robertsons' work on separation, and one practical result has been the institution of easy visiting and rooming-in in some children's hospitals. In regard to the further application of this research, it could be claimed that one reason why fostering became quickly accepted in the post-war years, in place of the large institution, was that fostering is much cheaper and, for this reason, receives Treasury support at top level.

The price of ignoring known things about delinquency is to be measured in terms of the cost to the community. But there is a positive feature here: the Children Act, 1948, which is preventive medicine in respect of delinquency, perhaps the best single thing in the whole vast area that I am examining.

Dividends

It is not my intention to be wholly pessimistic. Just as Freud has permeated life, literature and the visual arts, so have the many principles of dynamic psychology had their effect on infant and child care, education, and on religious practice: everywhere the analyst's researches have strengthened the hands of those who think in terms of the emotional growth of the individual and those who think of health in terms of the journey of the individual from dependence to independence, and of the progress of the child towards becoming gradually and in due time (i.e. after and not during adolescence) identified with society, taking part as an adult in society's maintenance and alteration.

In time it will be accepted that the findings of psychoanalysis have been in line with other existing trends towards a concept of society that does not violate the dignity of the individual. It will be found, if the world survives the next few decades, that the unpopular idea of unconscious motivation has been an essential element in society's evolution, and that psychoanalytic research will have played its part in saving the world from what, without the concept of unconscious motivation, must be fate. It would be nice if unconscious motivation could be generally accepted and studied before the time comes when fate will change its spelling to become *fait accompli*.

This Feminism

Draft of a talk given to the Progressive League, 20 November 1964

This is the most dangerous thing I have done in recent years. Naturally, I would not have actually chosen this title, but I am quite willing to take whatever risks are involved and to go ahead with the making of a personal statement.

May I take it for granted that man and woman are not exactly the same as each other, and that each male has a female component, and each female has a male component? I must have some basis for building a description of the similarities and differences that exist between the sexes. I have left room here for an alternative lecture should I find that this audience does not agree to my making any such basic assumption. I pause, in case you claim that *there are no differences*.

My subject is, in any case, a vast one, and I cannot cover what I know, or think I know. The thing that may be important to any one person may be hiding in among the things I shall have to leave out.

Developmental Approach

Naturally, I tend to look at this subject in terms of the development of the individual, development from the word 'go' to the time of death from old age. Development is my special line of country. I shall not worry whether man is more beautiful than woman, or whether there is a use for 'pretty' on the female side which demands on the male side another term, such as 'rugged'. All this must be left to the poets.

Actually (if you know what I mean by 'actually'), men and women have their own shapes. It is very convenient when a boy wants, on the whole, to be a man, and when a girl, on the whole, wants to be a woman. However, this is by no means always what one finds. And if one takes into consideration the deeper feelings and the unconscious, one may easily find a tough male hankering after being a girl, and a girl who is having a terrific bed-life in adolescence all the time envious of males. In fact, every degree of cross-identification can be expected, and troubles come mainly from the way in which these awkward things can be truly hidden in the repressed unconscious. Worse troubles come from the way in which, in schizoid persons, a splitting of the personality may separate the male and female elements, or may separate whole-functioning from part-functioning.

Let me look at this in five arbitrary layers:

1. Most males become men and most females become women, but then we need to consider the various kinds: heterosexual, homosexual or bisexual.

2. Adolescence has a slow tempo and, in the course of these five or so years, we must expect teenagers to play with all the variants before settling down to be male males and female females.

3. Prepuberty is an age at which a big proportion of children show a temporary swing to the sex opposite from their own.

4. Earlier, in the latency period, no one minds much if a girl wears jeans, but for some reason, boys are expected to look like boys and to do boyish things, like fighting and ganging up. But boys can be maternal and creative if they want to be, nowadays. Fashions change, and no one can predict for the next decade.

5. Earlier still, the crucial age of late toddlerdom finds most children (except those who are boiling up for psychiatric

disorder) in an acute stage of attraction to the parent of the opposite sex, with tension in relation to the parent of the same sex because of ambivalence – that is, coexisting love and hate. Some find, and some do not find, a corresponding element in the parent.

Here we assume a fantasy life; these children dream, they play, they imagine and use the imagination of others, and their total lives are very rich and their feelings are violent. Obviously much depends here on chance phenomena; for example:

A boy may love his father, who is shy and cannot respond because his natural homosexuality is under repression. The boy may then become father-deprived. This cramps his heterosexuality because he cannot let himself go when in a hate relation to his father.

Or a girl loves her father, but mother belittles all men and spoils the whole show. So the girl misses the boat with father, but catches it with her big brother.

A girl and boy suffer from the fact that the girl is a year older and so the sexes ought to have been reversed.

A boy is the third boy in a family of four boys. This third boy gets all the parents' wish to have had a girl. He tends to fit into the assigned role, however much the parents try to hide their disappointment.

In other words, the nature of the parents, the place of the child in the family, and other factors all affect the pattern and distort the classical picture which is known as the Oedipus complex.

Then we go deeper, or earlier, to more primitive mechanisms. How do babies come to terms with their own bodies? Partly by experiencing the excitements. But boys who experience erections and girls who have vaginal stirrings in relation to persons and in relation to loving and in relation to the functioning of the body are in a different position from those boys and girls who have no such integrative experiences. A great deal depends on the parents' attitude to all natural phenomena. Some parents fail to mirror what exists; others stimulate what is only there in embryo form.

A Specific Detail

There is one detail that must be examined separately. This is the male organ's quality of being obvious, contrasted with the female organ's quality of being hidden. We cannot talk about feminism and leave this out.

Freud invented the concept of a phallic phase, preceding full genitality. One could call it the phase of swank and swagger. There is no doubt that girls do have a bit of bother when going through this phase, or what corresponds to it in the girl. Just for a while they feel inferior, or maimed. The trauma of this varies according to the external factors (place in family, nature of brothers, attitude of parents, etc.), but let it not be denied that in this phase the boy has it, and the girl hasn't. Incidentally, the boy can micturate in a way that girls may envy as much as they envy the boy's erection. Penis envy is a fact.

At the next phase of full genitality the girl is equalized; she becomes important and envied by the boys because she can attract father, because she can have babies (eventually – either herself or by proxy), and at puberty she has breasts and periods, and all the mysteries are hers.

But Freud insisted right to the end of his life that if we neglect the effect on girls at the phallic phase of the trauma of their own 'inferiority' we lose something important. (Some analysts have tried to show that Freud was wrong here, and that it was Freud who was swanking over women, and planting this complication on humanity for reasons of his own.)

The consequences of this trauma that girls sustain at the phallic phase are of the following nature:

1. Over-valuation of the erect penis in its display and dominance.

2. Envy of males among girls.

3. Fantasy of the hidden penis that will one day develop and show.

4. Fantasy that the penis was but no longer is.

5. *Delusion* in the girl that a penis exists, and denial of the difference between male and female at the phallic stage; and *delusion* in the males that the girl has a penis, only just hidden away. This contributes to the appeal of the can-can, strip-tease, etc.

All this feeds into the sado-masochistic organization, and some perversions are an elaborate attempt to bring about some kind of sex union in spite of the delusion that the girl has a penis.

Here is a root of feminism. I cannot help it if there is much else in feminism, and if logic can be brought in on the side of much that feminism does and says. The root of it lies in the generalized delusion, *in girls and also in men*, that there is a female penis, and in the special fixation of certain women and men at the phallic level, that is, at the stage before the attainment of full genitality.

Perhaps the worst part, sociologically speaking, is the male side of this mass delusion, because it makes men emphasize the 'castrated' aspect of the female personality, and this makes for a belief in female inferiority that infuriates females. However, do not forget (if there are feminists present) that male envy of women is incalculably greater, that is, man's envy of woman's full capacity, of which more anon.

It will be understood, I hope, that this is a universal problem, and that in the normal it is the same as in the abnormal, only there is no elbow-room in the abnormal – in psycho-neurosis – for play and for fantasy because of some degree of repression. That is to say, some aspects of the totality are unavailable for use in self-expression and for incorporation in the structure of personality development. It should be noted, however, that developmentally there needs to be some healthy growth to reach penis envy.

Feminism, then, can be said to have in it a bigger or smaller degree of abnormality. At one extreme it is woman's protest against a male society dominated by phallic-phase male swank; and at the other extreme it is a woman's denial of her true inferiority *at one phase* of physical development. You will understand that I know that this simple statement is inadequate, but perhaps it can stand as an attempt to gather much complexity into the compass of a few words.

Continuing to look at the matter developmentally, what state is the little girl or boy in as the phallic stage appears on the scene? It is regular for little children who have had rather poverty-stricken experiences at the early stages, at the breast for instance, to get excited at this second chance that the phallic phase seems to offer – true both of boys and girls. In this way one can categorize two groups; those boys and girls who reach the phallic phase after having had full-blooded experiences at the earlier stages, and those who come to it relatively or very much deprived. The phallic phase has exaggerated importance for those who come up to it already deprived. In this and other ways there is a prehistory to troubles at this or at any other phase, and of course I must not forget to mention pathological hereditary tendencies.

All these things are everyday matters for a psychoanalyst treating patients, and yet they are not of much value in general discussions (such as this one) that are unrelated to therapy. People have to accept what they are and the history of their personal development along with the local environmental attitudes and influences, and they have to get on with life and living, attempting to interweave with society in such a way that there is a cross-contribution.

In health these things that are fixed in abnormal conditions are all present, but ways are found for hiding the crude elements without too great a loss of contact with these crude elements. For instance, there is the use of fantasy.

Fantasy and Inner Psychic Reality

Fantasy means to some people a manipulated affair, rather like what a child's comic is to a child. But fantasy goes deep into the personal inner psychic reality, which is the vital part of the unit personality, except where illness determines that there must be no inside and therefore no inner psychic reality. It is a characteristic of maturity, and so of health, that the individual's inner psychic reality is all the time becoming enriched by experiences and all the time making the individual's actual experiences rich and real to them. In this way, everything under the sun can be found in the individual, and the individual is able to feel the reality of whatever is actual and discoverable.

In health, then, the woman can find a male life in imaginative experiences through identification with males. In the crudest form of identification the woman can use a male, and so get a bonus from handing over her maleness and experiencing what she has it in her to experience as a woman. The same can be said in terms of the male's use of a woman.

Envy of the Opposite Sex

This leads me to make the following formulation: *to fully appreciate being a woman one has to be a man, and to fully appreciate being a man one has to be a woman.*

Envy of the opposite sex gives a reason for much of the frustration in people who live lives that depend heavily on instincts, and this means most people between puberty and fifty. Relief from this sort of frustration comes from the cultural life, in which there is minimal sex-linkage.

Some marriages break at the end of the in-love period because cross-identifications become weakened, and then the man's envy of the woman's being a woman is well matched by the woman's envy of the man's being a man. So these two who were in love now start throwing plates at each other. In plate-throwing men and woman are equal. In the new partnership which may follow, cross-identifications re-establish themselves, and for a time there is a saving in crockery.

Children find it difficult to allow for these things in their parents, but this just can't be helped. The forces may be so strong that there just have to be casualties among the offspring when parents substitute plate-throwing for intercourse or separate to save the crockery.

It will readily be seen that an ever-so-sweet man can either drive the woman partner over into a tremendous need for a very male male, even a horrid male, a crude cruel male that no one likes or could like, or else can make her fall back on her own maleness, exaggerating the ingredients of her latent feminism. Yet maternal males can be very useful. They make good mother-substitutes, which is a relief to the woman when she has several children, and when she is ill, or if she wants to get back to her job. Also, a lot of women want their men to be able to be maternal to themselves. Who is not a little deprived in regard to mothering? And women's friendships cannot be fully exploited without fear of homosexual complications.

All this shows how difficult monogamy is in practice. Or is it impossible, a bit of Christian teaching that ignores too much? Yet people do want to find they have kept up an intimate relationship over a life-time, because there is so much to be gained from the accumulation of shared experiences. But if we watch people struggling, we see how much at a disadvantage they are if they have a relatively unimportant personal inner psychic reality, and therefore a relatively restricted fantasy elaboration of the actual, and a poorly developed cultural involvement. The cultural life helps when a husband and wife fall out of love and into the second phase of the marriage game.

Woman and Women

I now want to jump into a consideration of an aspect of this wide subject which is sometimes neglected. There is a difference between men and women which is more important than being at the sending or the receiving end in feeding or in sex. It is this: there is no getting round the fact that each man and woman *came out of a woman*. Attempts are made to get out of this awkward predicament. There is the whole subject of couvade, and in the original harlequin myth there is a man who gives birth to babies. And the idea of being born out of the head is often found, and it is certainly easy to jump from the word 'conception' to the concept of 'conceiving of'. A child is lucky if 'conceived of' as well as being the result of physical conception.

However, every man and woman grew in a womb and was born, even if by Caesarean section. The more this is examined the more it becomes necessary to have a term WOMAN that makes possible a comparison of men and women. I must be brief, and therefore I take the argument deeper by formulating two stages in our thinking.

1. We find that the trouble is not so much that everyone was inside and then born, but that at the very beginning everyone was *dependent* on a woman. It is necessary to say that at first everyone was *absolutely* dependent on a woman, and then relatively dependent. It seems that the pattern of your personal mental health and mine was laid down by a woman at the start who did what she had to do well enough, at the stage when love can only be expressed physically if it is to be meaningful to the baby. All are born with hereditary tendencies towards maturation, but for these to have effect there has to be a good-enough facilitating environment. This means sensitive initial adaptation on the part of a human being. That human being is woman, and usually mother.

2. Deeper than this is a baby's experience, which at the beginning involves this woman because the infant has not yet separated out the mother, the environmental provision, the sensitive holding and handling and the feeding, from the self. The self has not yet been differentiated. Hence, absolute dependence.

Now it is very difficult indeed for a man or woman to reach to a true acceptance of this fact of absolute and then relative dependence in so far as it applies to the actual man or woman. For this reason there is a separated-out phenomenon that we can call WOMAN which dominates the whole scene, and affects all our arguments. WOMAN is the unacknowledged mother of the first stages of the life of every man and woman.

Following this, we may find a new way of stating the difference between the sexes. Women have it in them to deal with their relation to WOMAN by identification with her. For every woman, there are always three women: (1) girl baby; (2) mother; (3) mother's mother.

In myth the three generations of woman constantly appear, or three women with three separate functions. Whether a woman has babies or not, she is in this infinite series; she is baby, mother and grandmother, she is mother, girl baby and baby's baby. This enables her to be very deceitful. She can be a sweet little thing to catch her man, and then become a dominating wife-mother, and later gracious grandmother. It's all the same because she starts off three, while man starts off with a tremendous urge to be one. One is one and all alone, and ever more shall be so.

Man cannot do this that woman can do, this being merged in with the race, without violating the whole of his nature. It can happen in illness. I know of a man (a patient) who very early identified himself with woman, indeed with the breast. His potency was a breast function. There were no males in his life, only himself 'in' with women and emasculated even by his own male physical functioning. But he was never in any way a contented person, and he took tremendous trouble, pursuing treatment for years, to reach his male oneness, and to achieve his separation from woman. Having found his unique male self, he became able to relate in a new way to other unique males – that is, to have male friends.

I would say that feminist women look as if they envy this

thing about men: that the more men mature, the more they are unique. Some men envy women the way they need not solve the problem of an individual relationship to WOMAN because they are woman as well as charmers and seducers and helpless females calling successfully on man's chivalry. (Cries of 'Where is the chivalry of yesteryear?')

The awkward fact remains, for men and women, that each was once dependent on woman, and somehow a hatred of this has to be transformed into a kind of gratitude if full maturity of the personality is to be reached.

The Danger Seekers

And now let me ask you to consider a new detail: why do males seek danger? It is fruitless to try to stop wars and road accidents and expeditions to Everest and to Mars or to suppress boxing without looking to see what men are up to.

Women – all of them by virtue of their identification with women of the past, present and future – go through the risk of childbirth. It is no good pretending that childbirth carries no risk, and twilight sleep does nothing to the main argument here, which is that there is a danger inherent in the woman's natural function. Men envy women this danger; moreover, they feel guilty because they cause pregnancies and then sit pretty and watch women going through it all, not only the childbirth, but the whole confinement and the terribly restricting responsibilities of infant care. So they take risks too, and they will always do so. Some feel compelled to take risks insanely. They are trying to break even. But when a man dies he is dead, whereas women always were and always will be. A man is as grass.

So men have their troubles too. The awful thing about war is that so often those men who survive have to admit they found maturity, including sexual maturity, in the course of taking the risk of dying. So with no more wars, males find themselves high and dry; yet they hate getting killed, unless sure of the cause.

Tailpiece

I have roved round the subjects that cluster about the word
'feminism' and that belong to universal male–female inter-
actions. There is much else to be said, but this is not a matter
for shame. The more we look the more we see.

The Pill and the Moon

[The talk that follows was given to the Progressive League on 8 November 1969. It has survived only in the form of a recording of the event itself, and the reader will be aware of the informality of its language. Dr Winnicott always enjoyed addressing the Progressive League and they enjoyed listening to him; this is evident on the tape from the laughter and the noises of an audience very much alive. Unfortunately, in a few places these noises have obscured some of the words spoken by him, and a further difficulty arises from the fact that repetitions of words and of phrases occur, as well as interjections possibly due to a hesitancy in approaching in public a subject at once so difficult and, at bottom, so serious. There has therefore been a need for a certain amount of editing; but as this has consisted mainly in telescoping, no words or phrases are used that were not used by the speaker himself, and the order of the material has been strictly adhered to.

The talk was originally simply called 'The Pill'. However, the dream told by Dr Winnicott at the end of it, as well as his closing words, seemed to lead naturally on to the poem he wrote about the Moon Landing of July 1969. This is therefore included at the end, and the title has been altered in its honour. – Eds.]

Actually, you know, I've never had the Pill. And I know really very little about it. But when I was asked to talk about it, the *idea* was simply marvellous, and at the beginning it seemed to be exactly what I wanted to do, to talk about the Pill and the Progressive Me.

I find that what I'm lacking is some kind of propaganda

slant. It's lovely if you've got one and you really can go to
town on it, and hope that as a result of what you're saying no
one will ever take the Pill again, or that everyone will take it.

I did commit myself once a few years ago in something I
wrote in *New Society*[1] on the subject of going through the
doldrums, which is mainly about adolescence, but of course
it was quite an advanced essay in those days because things
change so quickly, don't they? About ten years ago people
were saying that the Pill is very soon going to be moderately
safe and available and it's going to alter the adolescent scene,
it's going to alter the scene for all parents. Well, it has done,
and you can hardly remember when it didn't alter the scene.
What is interesting is to think of how this is fitted into the
scheme of things imaginatively. I would guess that we haven't
really done our homework on the imaginative side of it.

Well, I settled down the other day – I had very few patients
– and I sat on the floor, which is the best place to sit, with a
biro in my hand and a piece of paper, and I thought to
myself: now I'll just sketch out what I'm going to say on
Saturday. That's easy, because I know what I want to say, I
know the limits and the things you put down, a, b, c and so
on. And nothing happened, all day! The only thing that
turned up was a poem. And I shall read it to you because it
surprised me, but I can't write poetry, so really it's absolutely
useless. I've called it, 'The Silent Kill'.

> O silly Pill for folks not ill!
> Why not wait till you know God's will?
> What's empty will in time refill
> And pregnant hill be razed to nil.
> Men! have your will, put Jack in Jill;
> Girls! drink your fill of his chlorophyll.
> Fear not the spill you know the drill,
> You know a still and silent kill . . . the Pill.

1. 25 April 1963. See also 'Adolescence: Struggling Through
the Doldrums', in *The Family and Individual Development*,
London, Tavistock Publications, 1965. [Eds.]

So take my quill I surely will:
Don't dally dill with silly Pill,
Just wait until what happens will!
Then pay the bill.

So that was something I'd got in my mind as I started to write. It reminded me of making something with a piece of wood. It's as though you thought: I'll make a sculpture in wood, and you got a gouge and a bit of elm, and you went like this and like that, and suddenly you found you'd got a witch in front of you. It wouldn't mean that you'd thought of a witch, but that the activity in the medium altered what you were doing, so that you surprised yourself. You found you'd done a witch because the elm made the thing go that way. You can translate this into any terms you want – in any art form – even if it turns out to be a silly rhyme like mine. It makes you surprise yourself, because you've done something you weren't expecting. So let's put the poem on one side, and see what happens to it.

Now we come back to the other side of things: logic, conscious logic. Such a lot of our life is frankly boring and ever so simplified, because we forget the unconscious, leave it aside, or only have it on Sunday morning. We work out what is the logical thing, and we have to. We're civilized people, we use our intellects and our minds and our objectivity. We've got the capacity to look and see how many people are going to be in the world in the year 2000, and exactly on what date India will be solid. And we don't have to go to India. We can think of the date on which London will be solid – we're already doing it in terms of the motor car.

So we can think in terms of the logic of the situation: is it logical to have enormous families apart altogether from whether people can afford to bring them up, and is it logical to fill our country with too many children? And we can say: 'No it isn't, no.' All right then, we'll only have two children each, every couple, or only have three in case one is a mongol or dies of polio; and then you could say: 'Let's have four then, just in case I wanted a boy badly, and had three girls in a row.' Anyway, it creeps up again, and very soon you've got back to where you were at the beginning, when you go on having them when they turn up. And maybe you find you're beginning to get a slant on your inhibitions – your sexual inhibitions, which perhaps result in there being no children at all – and you suddenly find that you're talking about the purely unconscious. In a sense the sexual inhibitions are just as interesting and just as constructive and just as much a contribution to society as sexual compulsions, so that we're all just describing each other and hoping to come out of it not too badly.

You have thought about the subject a very great deal, and I don't have to fill in the things you know. We're talking about world population, we're talking about ability to earn money and to bring up children, and whether we're willing to just put them in the education pool, or whether we have to be able to send them to what we consider to be a school which suits that particular child but might not suit anybody else. The whole thing is a matter of thinking things out, and thank goodness we've got brains, and we *can* think things out and we can act on what we think out. The logic of it takes us right down to the fact that it is necessarily sound that we don't deal with unlimited children, and somebody might say this even when they've had twelve children. There's some sort of way of working with this matter of thinking things out and of what actually happens, and we notice that the correlation between them isn't very high. We think things out and we see what happens and the two things are related in a new sort of way.

So now let's look at a case. It's the case of a girl of sixteen, and what she wanted from me was to be told that she was injured at birth. She started off with a handicap, being extremely blue at birth because the cord was round her neck. She nearly died, and when she came round no doubt a lot of damage had been done to brain cells. She wasn't very damaged – she simply had a limited depth to her personality which she had been struggling with all her life. As soon as she went to any sort of school everybody was always saying: 'If you tried harder you would be able to do this better.' So she tried and she tried and she tried, but nobody said to her: 'This is all a bit irrelevant.' She was extremely handsome and attractive, this sixteen-year-old, and naturally very forward emotionally. When she came she'd got a book with her, and she said, 'I'm reading this and I find it very interesting'; and it *was* an interesting book. But you knew she had trouble seeing into it what you and I would see into it, because she just can't get to it, hasn't got it, not quite.

We played squiggles together, to and fro, and one of her squiggles obviously had to be made into a head and a body, and there was a thing on the squiggle which was a cord, and I said, 'There's a cord round that child, there's a rope around that person's neck.' This came by chance through playing like that, you see; and we went on playing. Then she said to me, 'By the way, I was born with a cord round my neck.' She'd been told this. And I said, 'Oh look, we've got a drawing of that.' And she said, 'Oh, have we?' She hadn't thought of it in that way. But it turned up in the play material just like that, and when I made enquiries I found that this was actual fact and not just family saga. So we got on to this fact and I said, 'Look,' (I didn't protect her at all) 'you were born with this thing round your neck, you were blue and you were damaged at birth and you've been struggling to get on in spite of that. You've got a limited brain capacity, but that sometimes does improve as time goes on, and if you can wait you may find you'll be able to do something about it – I don't know yet. But the fact is that your trouble isn't that you aren't trying hard, it is that you're carrying around a damaged brain with you.' And she went home, and her reaction was to say to people: 'I feel somebody's understood me at last.' Out of a tremendously complex situation just that one thing emerged, and from there she's gone ahead in a different sort of way. We formed an extremely good relationship, and she can use me now, and I'm having her looked after so that she can live a normal life without anybody expecting her to do what she can't do because it needs a depth of achievement in her personality and in her intellectual capacity which is beyond her.

She has a terrifically acute crisis every so often, and when this happens it upsets the family and everybody around – even the animals. Her parents can't keep her at home because, though they're terribly fond of her, they can't stand the household being suddenly disrupted when she has come to the end of her capacity to tolerate things. So I was rung up one day and asked to see her. I saw her immediately, and this was the acute crisis (now we come back to the Pill). She went to a party. She tried not to go to parties, because she's very attractive and somebody notices her immediately and then in ten minutes they're having a marvellous time and the party's simply gorgeous, but what happens afterwards? She hasn't got the capacity to hold it. She's got very strong ideas of what she likes and what she doesn't like and what she thinks is right and wrong, and also very powerful instincts. But this time, she found a man she liked. This was the important thing, which made it very difficult for her to refuse him. So after the party, if she didn't go to bed with him she wouldn't know at all how to deal with the frustrations and the whole thing and she hasn't got the capacity to deal with it in her dream work or in other ways. She did stay all night, but she refused him, and he respected it. But she was absolutely torn with the disappointment that he hadn't raped her and taken full responsibility, and with the other thing that was her respect for him, because she knew that if his friends found that he'd spent the night with her and hadn't had intercourse, they would despise him. So he was left having to go home to where he lived and either tell a lie or say: 'Well, she didn't want it'; and that was going to be no good. She respected all this, and she felt absolutely torn, and was in a most terrible state and upset the whole family, who didn't know where they were except that they're used to this sort of thing. Incidentally, he was a very black African, which didn't seem to make any difference in their family. This wasn't the heart of the problem, though it was very exciting for her to have a black man. But that's another matter for discussion.

So this man behaved well, and she was frantically upset about it because he'd behaved well, and yet tremendously relieved; she was torn in a conflict that she couldn't contain.

Then she said, 'You see, the trouble is it hasn't got anything to do with sex, it's got to do with the Pill. All my friends have got the Pill. If I can't get the Pill I feel inferior and childish.' Her parents had said that she's not to have the Pill or any contraceptive until she's started with a new person she's going to live with and have some treatment. Her parents thought it was a good way of putting it off and so they said: 'No Pill yet for you, and no contraceptives; you've just got to contain yourself.' Really, the point about this girl was that the Pill was a terrific status symbol at her age of sixteen. If she was having the Pill she would be all right. These people feel that if something were different, then everything would be all right. She said, 'If I had the Pill, I wouldn't take it, you know, but I simply must have it. And if they say, you can't have the Pill, you're only sixteen, I've got to go and get it. I can get it and then I'll take it and that's the end of it.' And this is what she's like because it's all exaggerated by the fact that she hasn't got this depth of inner reality to help her work things out. When she started at this place where she's going, which is a rather good and understanding place, she came to see me one day and she said, 'I've had the most *lovely* day of my life.' And I said, 'What *did* you do?' I thought she must have had a series of black men! She said, 'We went down a lovely little stream and we caught tadpoles.' Yet from her point of view, not having the Pill and not being allowed the Pill was something she couldn't deal with. Everything was exaggerated. It seems to me that we can sometimes look at things in that sort of way, and see.

I want to think of one more case. A very intelligent woman, who was a deprived child, really, comes to see me regularly. She was married and has got children, but now she's divorced

and she's very lonely. As a result of some improvement because of treatment, she began to loosen up a bit, and so a man
asked her out to dinner. Okay, she's free now, she can go out
to dinner, she felt quite happy about that, she rather liked
him. And then, of course – I don't know how it happens –
but somehow or other they found themselves in a room somewhere. She said to me, 'I don't know what people are thinking
of these days; in 1969 they seem to think people live on the
Pill. I haven't thought about sex for ten years, and I don't
live on the Pill. He came without any contraceptives, so of
course, I had to fall back on the old thing, menstruation.' But
the idea was completely strange, you see. She was saying:
what an extraordinary thing. Here's a man who wants to
sleep with a woman and assumes she's on the Pill. It's the
language of 1969, isn't it? Both these things belong to a
sort of logical way of looking at it, even though this woman
has tremendous depth and could look at it in different
ways.

What I want to do is to see if I can show you that from my
point of view, there's an unresolved area in which logic and
feelings, unconscious fantasy and so on, don't tie up. They
don't relate to each other properly, they don't solve each
other, and there have got to be both; and we have got to
tolerate the contradictions. Of course, we can solve any problem by going off into the split-off area of the intellect. Up
there, somewhere, we are free from feelings; we can just say,
'dialectic'; we put this against that and then we can solve any
problem there is. Or if we can't we will be able to. But if we
don't go off into the split-off intellect, don't you feel that
we've got to say: 'Right, there are problems that can't be
solved, and we've got to tolerate tensions'? This is what I'm
trying to illustrate with the girl who was restricted because
her head was damaged at birth. She found it difficult to
tolerate the tensions that have got to be carried round with us
and that make us doubtful about everything and that make
us value doubt. Because certainty and sanity have a terribly
boring sound. Of course, insanity is boring too, but never-

theless, there's something that most people can tolerate to some extent, which is – uncertainty.

The thing I want to get to now is a startling thing, only you've already said it to yourselves, so I'm not saying anything famous or original. I'm saying that we are talking about the killing of babies. We're not talking about killing babies because they're not normal, because they're mongols or spastic or defective. Immediately we protect these, they have special care, we help each other with it. We're talking about the killing of babies apart from this complication. It's a very difficult subject and immediately we find we don't want it in the way. We're talking about the logic of Malthus, and the common sense of it, and we don't want to be bothered with all that. But I am asking, don't we have to be bothered with it?

When I was a little boy and had mice, if I handled the baby mice, the mouse just said: 'All right, I'll take them back'; so she just ate them and started again. Cats do that too. I don't think dogs do, but they've been trained for a million years not to be wolves, so that they've been domesticated unless they have rabies. It seems to me my pet mouse was solving the problem when she said: 'I don't need a Pill, because if I think that these babies aren't going to have a proper environment to grow into, that there's a stink of hands from that boy, well, I'll just eat them and start again.' Quite simple. I believe, only I'm not quite sure, because these things get caught up with mythology so easily, that Australian aboriginals at one time used to eat some of their children.[2] This was their way of solving the population problem. And the eating wasn't because they hated the children. What I am talking about is that when the environment is not seen to be sufficient to cope with the number of children, some or other method is found. The world up to recently has had a very good method indeed. People just died like flies of dysentery and other things, but now doctors have come along

2. Eating of the first-born by tribes in New South Wales is mentioned in J. G. Frazer's *The Golden Bough*. [Eds.]

and said: 'You needn't die of dysentery, you needn't die of malaria, you needn't die of any disease or epidemic at all.' So the population has to be thought of another way, because we can no longer leave it to God, so to speak, to kill everybody, though of course we can have a war and people can kill each other off that way.

If we're going to be logical, we're going to talk about a very difficult subject, which is: what babies do we kill off? Babies start to be human at what age? Most people agree that when they're born at full term, they're human beings. So we won't kill them. So then we talk about just before birth and we say: 'We won't kill babies that are viable.' Well, we go to the doctors and we say: 'At what age is a baby viable?' And they say the baby is viable at such and such a weight, four pounds, three pounds, two and a half pounds, and gradually it goes down like an auction. So we take the doctors' advice as to what is murder or not, then we go a little earlier and we say: 'That's all right. Abortion. We've decided.'

Just now I'm advising a girl who's happily married, but who's very restless indeed, and when her husband was drafted to the East I knew that this would be impossible for her to manage. So I wasn't surprised when she rang me up and said, 'Look, I'm pregnant, and I don't like the man and I hate the idea of breaking up my marriage and it's absolutely frightful.' I couldn't get in touch with the father immediately so I got the baby taken away. And everybody is logically extremely pleased that I did that, and the girl herself was ready for her husband when he came back, and they had two more children, and the home is not disrupted by having in it a little foreigner from some unwanted love affair which she couldn't help, because she hasn't got a deep capacity to tolerate things.

Now that's all quite logical. But what about the girl? She still feels absolutely awful about the murder of this child who was three months old inside her, but she can tolerate it, and I can talk about it with her and she knows that she feels awful about it. So it isn't just logic, is it? There's the murder. We're talking about something really tremendous.

If I go back further there's a girl who was asked to help in a mental hospital at the age of about eighteen. The mental hospital was very keen on helping all the young people in it, so they put her into close contact with a boy, a schizophrenic, and she did him a tremendous amount of good, I can promise you. Only, at the same time, she became pregnant. I think the mother thought it was very irresponsible of the hospital, and she stopped the girl going there and helping with the unit. And we said– 'Right, quickly this girl must have this baby taken away.' So I arranged it and I pushed forward, because what happens is that the doctors say: 'Let's think again'; and you come back in two months and the mother has already begun to orientate towards the baby, and it's now going to be traumatic to have an abortion. And very often it's too late, and then she has an unwanted baby to carry, and there's a baby in the world that wasn't wanted, and this is a terrible problem. Anyway, I rushed things to and fro, and I had everything by-passed, and the girl got rid of the baby before she had begun to orientate towards it. So she's all right and she's not feeling guilty about it, because this was done. Now she's planning to marry this ex-schizophrenic boy, and they're planning to have a family when they feel settled.

I'm asking for us to retain the emotional, fantasy side of the thing while still indulging in the extreme of logic, because I absolutely believe in objectivity and in looking at things straight and doing things about them; but not in making it boring by forgetting the fantasy, the unconscious fantasy. It's not very popular, you know. No one is more intolerant of unconscious fantasy than the general public. The extreme of logic gives us the Pill and the use of it, and I know this has made a tremendous amount of difference, and I can see that the world can make use of it. But I am suggesting that we are all dissatisfied if that's all we do about it, and that we've got to see that the Pill is what I called, 'The Silent Kill'. My so-called poem contains a good deal of conflict, it doesn't solve anything, but nevertheless it gets me quite unexpectedly to what I didn't know I was going to say at all – which is that in the imagination, the Pill is the silent kill of the babies. People have got to be able to have feelings about that.

I'm used to this subject, mind you, because of the fact that I'm dealing with children. Let's take the youngest child in the family. I've found that he – or she – has killed all the others that didn't come after him. For many of them, I find that they're dealing with terrific guilt feelings of having killed off all the other children. So we're quite used to all this if we're used to the fantasy that there is in children's lives.

You might think that I was saying: 'All right, we're going to find that the Pill is killing babies, so of course, we don't take the Pill.' But I'm not saying that at all. I'm just saying: 'So of course, we recognize that there are times when we say "yes", we kill babies. Only we do it terribly respectably.' It's not because we hate them – that isn't the point. We kill babies because we can't provide them with an environment that's right for them to grow up in. But we do get down to very primitive things to do with destruction, destruction that belongs to object-relating. Before hate, in a sense, object-relating involves destruction.

The trouble with me is that I find I can't orientate to a subject without gathering myself together and getting tense towards it, and when I'm talking about a subject anywhere, I, like other people, find myself dreaming about it. Last night I had two dreams. In the first I was at a conference. It wasn't like this – it was more like the Psychoanalytic Conference I didn't go to in Rome this year. There was a whole family there, men, women, children. There were a terrific number of people. And things were going all right, when suddenly, whoosh across the scene, came the daughter of the family. She came rushing in and she was telephoning all around the place and to the hotel, and saying, 'Mother's lost her handbag!' She said, 'I want you to understand this, she might find it again, but while she's lost it we've all got to be looking for it for her!' And so everybody downed tools – no conference, no anything at all – we were looking for mother's handbag.

So here is something we've got to tolerate, if we're thinking about the imaginative content of using the Pill. It unfortunately cannot be avoided that it involves the fantasy of the woman losing her womanliness.

The other dream I think was a male dream. It interested me because there was a most beautiful white object, and it was the head of a child. But it wasn't sculpted in any way: it was a two-dimensional representation of a sculpture. In the dream I said to myself: 'Look, the shading of dark and light on this is so beautifully done that we can forget whether it's accurate as a representation of a child's head and think about the further implication of it, which is the meaning of dark and light.' And in the dream, before I woke, I said: 'This has got nothing to do with the Negro problem of black and white – it goes right behind it. It has to do with the black and white that is in the individual human being.' And there it was.

And then I saw – because I get up quite a lot in the night at the moment, and I enjoy the moon so much – that of course it was the moon. And I knew it was the moon as well because it suddenly occurred to me: Oh damn, there's an American flag on it! And then I suddenly realized, when I began to get logical again, that we were back on the subject of menstruation and the woman who said: 'I had to go back and use menstruation again.' The fact is that here we're on to something extremely primitive to do with the moon and its tie-up with women and with the whole way the world has developed. I ended up by saying: 'The test of our civilization at the moment – the test is different from day to day – but the test today is: can we, as poets, recover from the American landing on the moon?' The song says: 'I gave you the moon, you'll get tired of it soon.' I'm tired of it already, absolutely. But when the poets begin writing about the moon again, as if it hadn't been landed on, but it meant things, like it means to you and me when we see it in the sky and the waxing and waning of it and the majesty of it and the mystery, then we

can get back to the time when we worked out what it all
means, when we knew what dark and light means. If we can
get back to the poetry and recover from the American landing
on the moon, before it starts up on Venus, we might feel that
there's some hope for civilization. That's a funny note I'm
ending on, when I'm really talking about the Pill. But from
my point of view, as I've never seen one, and I've certainly
never taken one, for all I know the Pill might look like the
moon. Perhaps that's my imagination.

Moon Landing

I

They say
They reached the moon
Planted a flag
    a flag stiffened of course
    (no gods breathe there)

II

Clever devils   I would fear
               I would panic
               I would doubt
               I would make a mistake
               I would faint
               I would leap, scream, laugh, go to
                  pieces.
Not so they.

III

What moon?
They made a room out of their heads
In a computer box they devised
Near-infinite complexity and then
Explored its finiteness. And then
They stepped on to it, planted a stiffened flag,

And took some marbles home, but not for children
to play with.

IV

Has anything altered?
Is this the shape of man's triumph,
    the mark of man's greatness
    the climax of civilization
    the growing point of man's cultural life?
Is this the moment for setting up a god
    who is pleased with his creative efforts?

V

No not for me
This is not my moon
This is not the symbol of cold purity
This is not the tide-master
Nor the phase-determinant of women's bodies
    the lamp fickle yet predictable to the
    shepherd astronomer that variably lights up
    the dark night or generates bats and ghosts
    and witches and things that go bump.

VI

This is not the moon of the magic casement,
Of the personal dream of Juliet of the balcony,
    (Nurse I come)

VII

My moon has no flag
no stiffened flag
Its life is in its active beauty
Its variable light
Its luminosity.

Discussion of War Aims

Written in 1940

The Prime Minister has seemed unwilling, much to the relief of many, to discuss war aims. We fight to exist.

Personally, I am not ashamed of the idea of just fighting to exist. We are doing no very extraordinary thing to fight simply because we do not wish to be exterminated or enslaved. *Le méchant animal, quand on l'attaque il se défend.* Ethics are not dragged in, and if we are fools enough to succumb, we shall not even have the chance to profit from our mistake.

If we fight to exist, we do not thereby claim to be better than our enemies. The moment we say we fight to possess, or to continue possessing, however, we introduce complications; and if we are rash enough to assert that we have some quality that our enemies lack, and which ought to be preserved, we have said something that we shall not find easy to justify. There is some point, then, in keeping our aims as simple as possible.

There is no clear reason why an ability to lead a country to victory should carry with it an ability to discuss war aims, and it may be important that we do not force the Prime Minister to do something out of character. What Mr Churchill is shy of doing, however, we who have less direct responsibility can do with profit. We can examine the possibility that we do stand for something valuable, and if we think we do, we try to work out just what that something may be. And when the words 'Democracy' and 'Freedom' appear in the discussion, we can try to understand what these words mean.

To clear the ground I would ask for acceptance as an axiom that if we are better than our enemies, we are only a little better. A few years after the war even this guarded statement will seem smug. In my opinion, it is no use pretending that human nature is fundamentally different in Germany and in Great Britain, although this, I admit, leaves me with the burden of explaining the admitted dissimilarity of behaviour in the two countries. I do believe that this dissimilarity can be explained, without the assumption that absolutely fundamental differences exist. It might be said, it is so obvious that behaviour is different here and there, and after all, is it not behaviour that matters? Well yes, but there is behaviour and there is total behaviour. Behaviour is one thing and total behaviour is another. Total behaviour includes historical responsibility; it also takes into consideration the widening of the basis of motivation through one's unconscious identification with one's enemies. Total behaviour also takes note of the capacity of the individual to get gratification in connection with ideas, perhaps aggressive or cruel ideas, and to derive relief when intolerable ideas that threaten to become conscious are acted out – that is, when the responsibility for them is shared by the other members of a group.

Put in a popular way, we may feel good, and we may behave well, but we need a yardstick for the awareness of goodness. The only really satisfactory yardstick for goodness is badness, and total behaviour includes this badness, even though it be our enemy who is bad.

At the present time we are in the apparently fortunate position of having an enemy who says, 'I am bad; I intend to be bad', which enables us to feel, 'We are good'. If our behaviour can be said to be good, it is by no means clear that we can thereby slip out of our responsibility for the German attitude and the German utilization of Hitler's peculiar qualities. In fact, there would be actual and immediate danger in such complacency, since the enemy's declaration is honest just where ours is dishonest. There, according to my view, is one of the reasons for his power to break up his opponents from within. He lures them into a position of righteousness which breaks down because it is false.

We very easily forget the fact that each time war comes along it has a value which is reflected in the course of politics. Peace is very difficult to maintain as a natural phenomenon for more than a certain number of years, and it would be possible to show that internal strains and stresses were appearing in the home political structure when the threat from abroad came along and gave us relief. (This does not mean that the war was engineered, as some say, to prevent revolution.)

In other words, human nature, called collectively the social structure, is no simple matter; and no help comes to the sociologist through his denying the power of greed and aggression that every individual has to deal with in his own self if he is to appear civilized. The easy way out for the individual is for him to see the unpleasant parts of himself only when these appear in others. The difficult way is for him to see that all the greed, aggression and deceit in the world *might have been* his own responsibility, even if in point of fact it is not. The same is true for the State as for the individual.

If we are willing to be educated, the events of the past decade have been eager enough to teach. A step in our education came from Mussolini, who said right out, before Hitler came on the scene, that the only justifiable possessing is that which is backed by physical strength. We do not have to discuss whether this is ethically right or wrong; we have only to note that anyone who is prepared to act, or even to talk, on this principle thereby forces everyone else to act on the same principle. Mussolini implied that Great Britain, France, Holland and Belgium were taking up a false position, claiming a right to territory as though God had so ordained, and it has been argued that even if his words only constituted a bluff, in forcing us once again to decide whether our position was or was not worth fighting for, he did us a good service.

If we accept the notion that basically in our natures we are like our enemies, our task is immensely simplified. We can then fearlessly look at our own natures, at our greed, and at our ability to deceive ourselves, and if on top of this we find that we do stand for something valuable to the world, we are in a position to see this in proportion.

It must be remembered that if we find that we do good things with the power we possess, this does not mean that we can possess without rousing jealousy. An enemy may be jealous of us not just because of our possessions, but also because of the opportunity which our power gives us for governing well and spreading good principles, or at the least for controlling the forces that might make for disorder.

In other words, if we acknowledge the importance of greed in human affairs, we shall find more than greed, or we shall find that greed is love in a primitive form. We shall also find that the compulsion to attain power can spring from fear of chaos and uncontrol.

What, then, can we put forward as a possible further justification for fighting which is primarily a fight for life? There is, in fact, only one way by which a claim that we are better than our enemies can be upheld without involving a never-ending discussion of the meaning of the word 'better'. It can be upheld if we can show that we aim at a more mature stage of emotional development than our enemies do. If, for instance, we could show that the Nazis are behaving like adolescents or preadolescents, whereas we are behaving like adults, we should have a good case. For the sake of argument I will say that the Mussolini attitude 'fight to possess' (if real and not just words) is relatively mature, and that the attitude 'surely you love and trust the leader' is normal only for the immature and preadolescent boy. According to this, Mussolini challenged us to behave as adults, while the Nazis challenged us as adolescents and they cannot understand us because they cannot see their own immaturity.

Probably our claim is that the Nazis are confidently preadolescent and that we are struggling to be adult. We are trying to feel free as well as to be free, and to be willing to fight without being pugnacious, to be potential fighters interested in the arts of peace. If we do claim this, we must be prepared to defend the claim and to understand what we mean by the words.

It is commonly assumed that we all love freedom and are willing to fight and to die for it. That such an assumption is untrue and dangerous is recognized by a few – who nevertheless fail, it seems to me, to understand what they describe.

The truth seems to be that we like the idea of freedom and admire those who feel free, but at the same time we are afraid of freedom, and tend at times to be drawn towards being controlled. The difficulty in understanding this is that the conscious and the unconscious are by no means identical. Unconscious feelings and fantasies give illogicality to conscious behaviour. Also, there can be a wide discrepancy between what we like when we are excited and what we like interim.

Interference with the exercise and enjoyment of freedom comes in two main ways. Firstly, the enjoyment of freedom only applies at all simply to the periods between bodily excitements. There is but little bodily gratification, and none that is acute, to be got out of freedom; whereas the ideas of cruelty or slavery are notoriously associated with bodily excitement and sensual experiences, even apart from actual perversion in which these things are acted out as a substitute for sexual experience. Therefore, lovers of freedom must be expected periodically to feel the seductive power of the idea of slavery and control. It may not be polite to mention the secret bodily pleasures and the thoughts that go with them, but the extraordinary lapses from freedom that history records cannot be explained under a conspiracy of silence and denial.

Secondly, the experience of freedom is tiring, and at intervals the free seek a rest from responsibility and welcome control. There is a well-known joke about a modern school in which a pupil says: 'Please, *must* we do what we want to do today?' Implied in this joke is a sensible answer, such as, 'Today I will tell you what to do, because you are a child and too young to take the full responsibility for your thoughts and actions.' But if it is an adult who asks the question, then we sometimes say: 'Yes, sir, you damn well must. This is freedom!' And probably he is willing to make an effort to exercise his freedom and even to enjoy it, provided he is given a holiday every now and again.

Here again, to feel free we must have a standard for measurement. How are we to be aware of freedom except by contrast with its lack? The enslavement of African Negroes provided and still provides us with a false easiness about our own freedom; and the reappearance of the slavery theme in our books, films and songs is largely our way of getting the feeling that we are ourselves free.

Our civilization has not yet tackled the problem of freedom apart from the existence of Negro slavery, if we include, as we must, emancipation of the slaves. Perhaps Germany was less involved than we or America were in these two experiences, which are one in total behaviour. This, if it were so, would make a lot of difference to the individual German's management of personal cruelty and the urge to control, giving him a greater need to act out in present day experience the cruelty and enslavement that the Americans acted out in the enslavement of Negroes and are still acting out through the great emancipation.

Freedom puts a strain on the individual's whole personality; the free man is left with no relief from any ideas he may have of being persecuted. He is left with no logical excuse for angry or aggressive feelings except the insatiability of his own greed. And he has no one to give or withhold permission to do what he wants to do – in other words, to save him from the tyranny of a strict conscience. No wonder people fear not only freedom, but also the idea of freedom and the giving of freedom.

To be told what to do affords a man great relief and only

demands his hero-worship of the person taking charge. At present we let Mr Churchill and certain others of his Cabinet tell us what to do in a most preposterous way that can only be explained by the assumption that we were all thoroughly sick of freedom and longing for a spell of slavery. In commerce, for instance, rules and regulations have been invented which are beyond the understanding of the small trader. He is first annoyed, and then becomes suspicious, and a number of the best of his kind are gradually being forced to give up, or are driven to physical or mental breakdown. The same can be said of many other departments. No doubt this has some value because of its cruelty and stupidity, which human beings put second in importance only to freedom. By linking freedom with peace and slavery with war and war effort, we have reached a happy state of affairs, which, however, depends on someone conveniently waging war on us. If we are stimulated to fight every two or three decades, we seem to be able to enjoy the practice of democracy and the experience of freedom.

It is quite a rare thing to meet an individual who is free and feels free, who can take responsibility for his actions and thoughts without over-frustrating himself, that is, without manifesting inhibition in excitement. Both inhibition and licence are easy, and both may be cheaply bought by giving over responsibility to an idealized leader or to a principle; but the result is poverty of personality.

Freedom being something that has to be forced on to those who are able to take it, a seer is needed to evaluate freedom and to show people it is worth fighting for and dying for, and this is true over and over again, generation after generation. Tolpuddle martyrs win freedom for their own generation, not for the trade-unionists of all time. The love of freedom will not of itself beget freedom. And the fact that men in slavery love the idea of freedom does not mean that they will love freedom when they are free. At first taste of it, at any rate, they are paralysed by it, fearing what they may do with it, as is well known. Then they come to terms with it, which means that to a greater or lesser degree they give it up.

It is difficult to feel free, and no less difficult to give others freedom. The war period provides us not only with a temporary relief from the strain of being free, but also it gives opportunity for dictators to have their little day. We have dictators all over the place, and they often do wonderful things which could never have been done in a parliamentary way. Aim having been agreed on, execution is merely a matter of efficiency. Will these men be fully gratified by the end of the war, and be contented to step aside and to allow the dawn of a new democratic day?

We are told that this war is being waged for freedom and I do believe some of our leaders can achieve this high aim. We are giving up as much of our freedom as Mr Churchill from time to time deems necessary. Let us hope there will be those who can feel free and tolerate the freedom of others when the battle is won.

Democracy is the exercise of freedom, and parliamentary government is the attempt to make freedom possible through the willingness of individuals to tolerate their opinions' eclipse if they are outvoted. This willingness to put up with not getting one's own way if one cannot get the support of the majority is a remarkable human achievement involving much strain and pain. It can only be possible if the gratification is allowed of a periodical illogical riddance of the leader. To give stability the king is maintained, illogically, permanent. In fact, the division of the head into the king and the prime minister is the essential of democracy. The American variation on this theme invests one man with permanence for a limited period.

It is really distressing to me to find democracy talked of at the present solemn time as if it just meant the State serving the people instead of the people serving the State. Surely the essential thing in democracy is that the people not only elect but also get rid of the leaders, and take responsibility for this. Feelings justify the change, though logic and reasoning are liable to rob these feelings of their crudity.

> I do not love thee, Dr Fell,
> The reason why I cannot tell . . .

Fortunately, human nature being what it is, some reason appears sooner or later to justify the removal of even the most loved and trusted chiefs; but the prime motive in the removal of a politician is subjective, and is to be found in unconscious feeling, so that if politicians get stuck, there becomes manifest a whole series of phenomena that cluster round unexpressed hate and ungratified aggressiveness.

A great threat to democracy in recent years came from the tendency of politicians to want to retire from old age, or to die in office, instead of suffering parliamentary defeat. Dying is not enough. A good House of Commons man, they say, is one who hits hard and expects to receive blows. What a happy chance it was for democracy that Churchill succeeded Chamberlain through parliamentary procedure, and not, as it would have appeared if Mr Chamberlain's removal had been postponed a couple of days, from our fear of the enemy attack!

In my opinion, the chief contribution of Lloyd George to the politics of the past two decades has been his playing the role of 'killed' chief, while all the other old men were trying to avoid being 'killed' by retiring unbeaten. Lloyd George had to be kept killed, and at times he must have felt himself to be wasted, when we can see that he was helping to preserve democracy from the rot which came from the politicians' fear of illogical removal.

The 'No Third Term' cry in the recent presidential elections echoed this same sentiment. Preservation of Roosevelt really might mean decay of democracy in the United States, since he must retire next time, and therefore no president can be sacrificed, illogically down'd, for at least eight years. The result must be a strengthening of the tendency to war or revolution, or to dictatorship.

The Nazis, who obviously enjoy being told what to do, need not feel responsible for choice of leader, and they are unable to throw him down, being in this respect pre-adolescent. We can claim that in the democratic way of life we aim at freedom, if we aim at a mature sharing of responsibility, especially the responsibility for illogical patricide, which we make possible by the splitting of our father-figure. But we must not be surprised when the others point out to us our failure to reach this freedom. We can only claim that we aim this way, or that as a nation we do achieve it for brief periods between wars. Indeed, personal freedom, the feeling of freedom, is too much to expect except of a few, a few valuable men and women of each era who do not necessarily achieve fame.

When it comes, then, to a statement of war aims, we can only be sure of one thing: that if we will survive, we must be willing to fight. We also claim that we hope to be more than willing to fight, for we try to practise freedom – which can give such dignity to the human animal. If we think we stand more than our enemies do for maturity of development, we have a strong claim to the world's sympathy, but we do not thereby avoid having to fight, or being willing to die if need be.

Our first aim is to win the war. Assuming we win, we are faced with the difficult task of first of all re-establishing our own freedom and our parliamentary system and democractic way of life, including the machinery for the illogical removal of politicians. This is our second war aim. Our third aim must be to seek out or be prepared to welcome the mature elements in the enemy countries. It is to be hoped that many of the Germans and Italians now showing defiantly adolescent mentality will be able to make a personal advance to maturity – that is, we may hope that many of them are now being lured back to adolescence or preadolescence rather than that they are fixed in an immature stage of development from personal inability to mature. For only in so far as the German people are mature can we usefully give them the idea of freedom.

To my mind, something more can be said of winning the

war, the first war aim. In this particular war, winning means calling the bluff to all propaganda. Our job is surely to put to the physical test everything which is thrown at us in words. It is for this reason that those who advocate propaganda from our side arouse in us more suspicion than admiration. There may be a place for propaganda as part of the war machine, but in this war it is important that we should win a military victory and not a moral victory.

The best hope for a period of peace is that the war should end at the moment when fighting ceases. If the side that wins has established supremacy in arms, the vanquished can still hold up the head. To fight and to lose is not worse for the soul than fighting and winning.

One could attempt to be extra clear by saying that if Germany wins, her victory must be by a superiority of fight and not of show, and if we win, as we confidently hope to do, this again must be because of superiority of fight.

If, however, an artificial peace is brought about before the supremacy of arms is established beyond doubt, then the old trouble about war guilt will crop up again, and the peace we all hope to know will be spoiled once more.

We hear little of the value of war, and no wonder, since we know so much about its horrors. But surely it is possible that the actual fighting, German versus Britisher, may tend gradually to foster maturity on both sides. We aim at reaching a saturation point when there is military satisfaction, and mutual respect between combatants, such as can never arise between propagandists and counter-propagandists, nor, I fear, between pacifists and pacifists. On mutual respect between maturing men who have fought each other, a new period of peace could be reached, perhaps lasting another couple of decades, till a new generation grows up and again seeks to solve or obtain relief from its own problems in its own way. Allocation of war guilt has no part in this scheme, since all share it, for peace spells impotence except it be won through fighting and the personal risk of death.

Berlin Walls

Written in November 1969

The Berlin Wall is the most notorious example of a phenomenon which can be found everywhere, but which gains special significance because of the fact that the world has now become one place and the human race has achieved some kind of unity.

There must be many ways of looking at this phenomenon in the world of practical politics and it would not be possible for one person to encompass the whole subject. Arising out of psychoanalytic practice, however, certain things seem to need to be said; two of these I wish to develop as separate themes.

The first has to do with the development of the individual unit. It is not possible to look usefully at the clinical state of a human being at any one moment. Much more profitable is the study of the development of that individual in relation to the environment, and this includes a study of the environmental provision and its effect on the development of the individual. The inherited maturational processes in the individual are potential and need for their realization a facilitating environment of a certain kind and degree, and there are important variations in the social environment according to place and time. It must be assumed that the world, in so far as it becomes a unit in sociological terms, cannot be better than the individuals that compose it. A diagram of the human individual is something that can be made and the superimposition of a thousand million of these diagrams represents the sum total of the contribution of the individuals that compose the world and at the same time it is a sociological diagram of the world. There is a complication here in that only a proportion of individuals achieve in their emotional development something which could be called unit status. Indeed, it is likely that the individual is a relatively modern concept and that there were no whole people until a few hundred years ago; or perhaps there were a few exceptional total individuals within the last two thousand years or so. It is only too easy nowadays to take for granted that the individual as a unit is the basis of everything human, and that any individual who has not achieved the integration into something that could be called a unit has not reached the baseline from which maturity can be achieved, whatever the word 'maturity' may mean.

The world, therefore, has to contain a proportion of individuals who cannot achieve integration into a unit and therefore cannot contribute, except destructively, to the world's integration. In pursuing this subject it is necessary to drop this complication and to look at the sociological world as the superimposition of millions of integrated individuals on each other. It can be assumed that in the world there will not be found anything better than can be achieved in the human being.

When we study the developing human babies and children and developing human beings in all groups all over the world, we find that integration into a unit does not mean that the individual has achieved peace. What the individual has achieved is a self which can contain the conflicts of all kinds that belong to the instincts and to the subtle needs of the spirit, and also the environmental conflicts which belong to the milieu. The diagram of the healthiest conceivable human being could be thought of as a sphere or more simply as a circle, and immediately it will be necessary to put a line down the centre. The individual with this degree of health is capable of containing all the conflicts that arise from within and without, and although there must always be war or potential war along the line in the centre, on either side of the line there become organized (by the integrative forces that belong to human development) groupings of benign and persecutory elements.

In the inner psychic reality which I am describing, there is not always war simply because of the line and the segregation of benign and persecutory elements. Help is afforded by the fact that benign elements can be exported, or projected, and so also may persecutory elements. In this way human beings are always inventing God and are always organizing disposal of dangerous or waste products.

There are two extremes clinically if one looks at human beings in the way they deal with these matters. At one extreme the whole of the conflict that the individual can know about is gathered together in the personal inner psychic reality. Total responsibility is taken for everything. Because of the danger if there is any movement, control of everything becomes automatically set up. The mood is then one of depression. At the alternative extreme the potential war in the inner psychic reality cannot be tolerated, and the individual looks for a representative of it in society, either local or general, and ultimately in the unified social concept of the world that we live in. In this way it is not only that there is always conflict in the social milieu, but also that conflict is invented and maintained by the individuals that compose society; and individuals not only suffer from the conflicts in the world around them, but also they get relief when conflict outside the individual gives relief from conflict within – that is to say, in the personal inner psychic reality.

Idealists often speak as if there were such a thing as an individual with no line down the middle in the diagram of the person, where there is nothing but benign forces for use for good purposes. In practice, however, it is found by all who study these matters that if the individual is almost free of the persecutory or 'bad' forces and objects, this simply means that some kind of scapegoat mechanism is at work, and that the individual is getting relief from a real or an imagined or a provoked or a delusional persecution.

In the same way it is impossible to conceive of someone who is all bad, whatever the word 'bad' may mean, that is to say, who contains only persecutory elements. This could be found in psychopathology, however, where in some cases of suicide the individual arranges to take all the bad within the self and to finish it after exporting or projecting what the individual feels to be the good. (One is reminded here of the end of the biography of Philip Hesseltine: he put out the cat, shut the door and turned on the gas.) It will be observed that in the depressed state which is probably part of the normal or psychiatrically healthy individual's personality structure, there is a toleration of the potential state of war. It is as if there is a Berlin Wall, or what is at present being called the army's peace line in Belfast. These are parochial matters, and by the time this paper has found a reader they may have been forgotten because of some other and better example of a dividing line, which at its worst postpones conflict and at its best holds opposing forces away from each other for long periods of time so that people may play and pursue the arts of peace. The arts of peace belong to the temporary success of a dividing line between opposing forces; the lull between times when the wall has ceased to segregate good and bad.

In all localities there is in the background a political issue, and the temporary solution of this issue, which involves war or civil war, is the basis for the episodes of peace and cultural achievement. This is the same subject as the well-appreciated fact that there are special conditions which make an island (if it is not too big) a place where the arts of peace can be practised. In other words, if a community is not also an island, it has frontiers and at the frontiers there is a state of strain. The behaviour of those who are on either side of the frontier determines the nature of the life of the people, and here again it is immediately clear that the toleration of antagonism without denial of the fact of antagonism is productive in a positive way; at the same time toleration of antagonism is the most difficult thing in politics. It is always easier to become strong and to push the frontier a little bit further away or to push it right over the heads of the people and to dominate the social group so that there is no freedom for that group, although there is freedom for the larger and stronger group that has achieved domination.

This is a reflection of the sort of thing that can happen in the individual when infatuation with a leader or an idea gives the individual absolute certainty of action and makes the individual into a dictator with no doubts and no hypochondria and no depression, only a compulsion to maintain domination. This is domination of good over bad, but the definition of good and bad belongs to the dictator and is not a matter for discussion among the individuals that compose the group and is therefore not constantly in revision in regard to meaning. To some extent it could be said that the dictatorship breaks down because the fixed meaning of good and bad eventually becomes boring, and people become willing to risk their lives in the cause of spontaneity and originality.

One can immediately begin to apply these matters to any small problem one can meet; for instance, if the wall in Northern Ireland is between Catholicism and Protestantism, this means there is no room for a healthy agnostic. Everyone in Northern Ireland at the present time must be Protestant or Catholic, although even the meaning of Protestant and Catholic will not be open for discussion but may be fixed by the historical roots which can give it a local meaning specific to Northern Ireland. In one respect it can be said that Northern Ireland is the permanent Berlin Wall between Eire and England. If Eire were to include the whole of Ireland, then the wall would shift into the water that separates the two islands. Actually, there is little doubt but that it would become an irregular line dividing populations in Glasgow, Liverpool and other areas in the west of this island, and this could mean also an exacerbation of Protestant–Catholic tension in London.

At the present time in London, as in Great Britain generally, the fixed state of Protestant colour makes for easy tolerance of Catholicism. In the same way, in Catholic Ireland there is easy tolerance of Protestantism, because Catholicism is assumed along with the climate. It is where the two climates of opinion meet that they clash.

It is not difficult to make statements of this kind in terms of other countries, although in every case anything stated briefly must be very poor in terms of truth, because the truth is complicated and therefore interesting and is rooted in history. Nevertheless, for purposes of illustration it is possible to take a certain amount of exercise stretching one's imagination as well as one's knowledge of some of the facts.

The common denominator of all these problems is the state of potential war that exists between factions which appear in couples. This theme, which is the theme that interests me while I am writing this, has to do with the meeting place between the factions and the organization at the place where the boundaries meet or where they would meet if it were not for the no man's land between the two boundaries. Much of what we call civilization becomes impossible the nearer we get to the customs barrier, so much so that we who travel with passports marvel at the ease with which the farmer may be ploughing his field and crossing the border many times a day, hardly noticing it, whereas if we were to follow him, we would be shot. Where the farmer cannot play with the border in this way, then we know that a state of potential war exists in that area, and we do not look for the arts of peace and for playful creativity there.

It is interesting to compare the rich developments that have come from the existence of the border between England and Scotland, although there is but little to indicate where England starts and Scotland finishes, or vice versa. We enjoy the gradual change of accent and the emphasis on history which has a different colour a little further north or a little further south. Undoubtedly the narrowness of this part of the island south of Edinburgh helps, so that we more or less feel we are in Scotland when we are in Scotland without anyone telling us.

The border between England and Wales has to be looked at in terms of geography and mountains. The boundary between East and West Berlin is a man-built wall which must be ugly, because there is no meaning of the word 'beauty' which could be connected with the recognition that here, exactly at this spot, is the place where if there is no wall there is war. But the positive thing in favour of the Berlin Wall is the acknowledgement of the fact that human nature is not capable of a totality except in terms of the depressed mood and of the acknowledgement of conflict in the inner psychic reality of the individual, and of a willingness to postpone resolution of the conflict and to tolerate the uncomfortableness of the mood. Naturally, in terms of time one can see that there is an alternation between resolution of the conflict, which means war or conquest, and toleration of the state of strain, which means acceptance of a Berlin Wall or its equivalent.

This is the manic-depressive psychosis in terms of time and of sociology, which is the same thing as the manic-depressive psychosis of alternating mood in the individual, which in turn is the same thing as the depressed mood of a total person who accepts the fact of conflict in the personal inner psychic reality.

Freedom

An amalgamation of two papers written around 1969

There is a place here for a statement on the meaning of freedom. No attempt will be made to view the vast literature both inside and outside psychoanalysis that deals with this idea. It is not possible, however, to shirk responsibility for taking a new look at the idea of freedom in the light of the concepts of health and creativity that I am emphasizing.

The subject of freedom has already been introduced when I refer to the environmental factor rendering creativity useless or destroying it in an individual by producing a state of hopelessness.[1] This is the subject of freedom in terms of the lack of it and the cruelty that is involved in either physical restraint or in the annihilation of an individual's personal existence by dominance, as, for instance, in a dictatorship. I have pointed out that such dominance can be found at home and not only in the wider political scene.

It is well known that stout persons throughout the ages have found that they had some sense of freedom, even an enhanced sense of freedom, when in states of physical restraint. Elsewhere I have quoted the well-known lines: 'Stone walls do not a prison make nor iron bars a cage.'

In terms of the individual who has a measure of psychiatric health, a sense of freedom is not altogether dependent on an

---

1. 'Creativity and its Origins', in *Playing and Reality*, London, Tavistock Publications, 1971; New York, Basic Books, 1971; Harmondsworth, Penguin Books, 1985.

environmental attitude. Indeed, it is possible for people to feel frightened of freedom when they are given it after it has been disallowed. This is something that has been observed in the political scene during the last half century, when so many countries have at last attained freedom and have not known what to do with it.

In a book that is not mainly concerned with politics, the study must be of the sense of freedom that belongs to the psychiatric health in the individual. Those who meet psycho-analytic theory for the first time not infrequently feel that however interesting it may be, there is some aspect that is frightening. The very fact that there can be a theory of the emotional development of the individual in relation to the environment and that the theory can be extended to explain disturbances of development and illness states makes many people actually disturbed. In lecturing to groups of mature students on the emotional development of the child and on the dynamics of mental disturbance and of psychosomatic disorder, one expects, from time to time, to get the urgent question that has to do with determinism. It is true, of course, that there is no theory of emotional states and of personality health and disorder and of behaviour vagaries unless there is at the basis an assumption which is deterministic. It is not helpful if the lecturer tries to make allowance for some area somewhere or other that is outside determinism. The study of the personality which is particularly associated with the work of Freud, which has led to an immense forward stride in man's attempt to understand himself, is an extension of the theoretical basis of biology, which in itself is an extension of the theoretical basis of biochemistry, chemistry and physics. There is no sharp line anywhere in the theoretical statement of the universe if one starts with the theory of the pulsating star and ends up with the theory of psychiatric disorder and of health in the human being, including creativity or seeing the world creatively, which is the most important evidence we have that man is alive and that the thing that is alive is man.

It is obviously very difficult for some human beings, and

perhaps for all human beings, to accept determinism as a basic fact, and there are many well-known escape routes kept open. Always if one looks at one of these escape routes, one can feel some hope that the route will not be blocked. For instance, if one looks at extra-sensory perception, one can see an attempt to prove that there is such a thing, but one can feel ambivalence in regard to the outcome, since if it is proved to exist, then immediately an escape route out of determinism is blocked and the result is another example of gross materialism. Materialism is not pretty, or agreeable in any sense, but neither can we say that we all wish to stand permanently looking for an escape route from determinism.

The lecturer in dynamic psychology who repeatedly meets this objection to his whole subject from a student who is disturbed by the determinism that is implied soon gets to know that this problem does not affect all the students all the time. In fact, the majority of people are not bothered by understanding, as far as it can be understood, that there is a deterministic basis to life. Suddenly the subject becomes vitally important to a student or it may become vitally important to anyone for a few moments, but the fact is that the majority of people for most of the time feel free to choose. It is this feeling of being free to choose and of being able to create anew that makes the deterministic theory irrelevant: mostly we feel free. Determinism can be just simply a fact of life that can feel uncomfortable from time to time.

What cannot be ignored is the fact that quite a big proportion of people, men, women and children, do feel intensely disturbed by something, and this can easily take the form of a revolt against determinism. We must look and see what this fear is and take it seriously. The feeling of freedom contrasts so greatly with the feeling of not being free that a study of the contrast becomes imperative.

There is one simple thing that can be said about this complex subject and that is that psychiatric disorder itself does feel to be a kind of prison, and a psychiatrically ill person can feel more confined in illness even than a person who is actually in prison. Some way has to be found for understanding what it is that the ill person describes in terms of lack of freedom. There is a way of looking at this question which belongs to the well-worn theories that arise out of psychoanalytic practice. It has to be remembered that whereas there is a vast amount for psychoanalytic theory to learn in respect of health, there is a great deal it does already know about in terms of illness. It is helpful in probing into this problem to make a statement of psychiatric health and ill health in terms of the defences that become organized in the human personality. These defences take various forms, and they have been stated in all their complexity by various psychoanalytic authors. It is true, however, that defences are an essential part of the structure of the human personality, and that without the organization of defences there is only chaos and organization of defences against chaos.

The concept that is helpful here is that in psychiatric health there is a *flexibility* of the defence organization, whereas in psychiatric ill health, by contrast, the defences are relatively rigid. In psychiatric health, for instance, there can be detected a sense of humour as a part of the capacity to play, and the sense of humour is a kind of elbow-room in the area of the defence organization. This elbow-room gives a feeling of freedom both to the subject and to those who are involved or who wish to become involved with the individual concerned. In the extreme of psychiatric ill health there is no elbow-room in the area of the defence organization, so that the subject is bored with his or her own stability in illness. It is this rigidity of the defence organization that makes people complain of a lack of freedom. This is a very different subject from the philosophic one of determinism, because of the fact that the alternatives of freedom and lack of freedom belong to human nature itself, and these problems are constantly urgent in everyone's life. They are particularly urgent in the life of the baby and the young child, and therefore in the lives of the parents, who are all the time playing around with the alternatives of adaptation and training, hoping to give the child the freedom of impulse that makes life begin to feel real and worth living and that leads to a creative view of objects and then leads on to the alternative, which is represented by teaching and by the parents' need to resume their own private lives, even at the expense of the child's impulsive gestures and claims for self-expression.

In our culture at the present time we are reaping the rewards of an era in which every effort is being made to give children, at any rate, the beginnings of a sense of freedom to exist in their own right, and some of the results of this are found to be uncomfortable when the child reaches adolescence. One can observe a social tendency to react in such a way that those who have responsibility for the management of difficult adolescents tend to question the validity of the theories which made a whole generation try to give children a good start. In other words, society is being provoked by freedom-loving people into harsh measures which eventually could build up into a dictatorship. This is the danger. Here are immense problems of management and a big challenge to the theory which is the backbone of our work.

The Threat to Freedom

Consideration of the concept of freedom therefore leads on to an examination of the threat to freedom. Such a threat certainly exists, and the only right moment for investigating this threat is before freedom is lost. In so far as freedom is a matter of the inner economy of the individual, it cannot easily be destroyed; that is to say, if freedom is looked at in terms of flexibility rather than rigidity in the defence organization, then it is a matter of the individual's health and not a matter of his treatment. Nevertheless, no one is independent of the environment, and there are environmental conditions which destroy the feeling of freedom even in those who could have enjoyed it. Certainly a prolonged threat can undermine the mental health of anyone, and, as I have tried to state, the essence of cruelty is to destroy in an individual that degree of hope which makes sense of the creative impulse and of creative thinking and living.

If one assumes that there is a threat to freedom, then one has to say that first of all the danger comes from the fact that those who are free both internally and in their social setting are liable to take freedom for granted. There is something comparable here with the need that exists to let mothers and fathers who are dealing with their babies and children satisfactorily know that what they are doing has importance as well as being enjoyable or at any rate satisfying. If things are going well, they take it all for granted and do not realize that they are laying down the foundations of the mental health of a new generation of people. They very easily get pushed sideways or backwards by any person with a system of thought, that is to say, anyone with some kind of conviction which must be spread or a religion to which people must be converted. It is always the natural things that get spoiled, just as the new motorway is placed exactly there in the isolation of the countryside where serenity could have been found. Serenity does not know how to fight for itself, but the anxious urge to push forward and to progress seems to contain all the dynamic. This idea is contained in the phrase of John Maynard Keynes, 'The Price of Freedom is Eternal Vigilance', which the *New Statesman* adopted as its motto.

There is a threat to freedom, therefore, and to all natural phenomena, simply because they do not contain the propaganda drive, and natural phenomena are overridden, by which time it is too late. We can do a little, therefore, by pointing out to free people the value to them of freedom and the sense of freedom, even going so far as to draw attention to the undoubted fact that feeling free may provoke the very restrictions from which they enjoy freedom. This of course refers to restrictions in the environment, but there is a limited value to inner freedom, which I have described in terms of flexibility of the defence organization, if it is only consciously experienced in circumstances of persecution.

On this basis it is interesting, if not valuable, to look at other reasons why there is a threat to everything that is natural. The suggestion I wish to put forward is that what we try to describe by saying that it is natural, if it concerns human beings and the human personality, has to do with health. In other words, the majority of people are comparatively healthy and they enjoy their health without being too self-conscious about it or without even knowing that they have it. All the time, however, there are the people in the community whose lives are dominated by some degree of psychiatric disorder or an unhappiness that they cannot account for, or a lack of any certainty that they are glad to be alive or that they want to go on living. I have tried to sum this up by saying that they suffer from a rigidity of defences. It is not always realized that here is something that goes deeper even than class distinction. It goes deeper even than the contrast between poverty and riches, although the practical problems associated with either of these two extremes produce such powerful effects that these effects dominate the scene only too easily.

When the psychiatrist or the psychoanalyst looks at the world, he cannot help seeing that there is this terrible contrast between those who are free to enjoy life and who live creatively and those who are not free in this way because they are all the time dealing with the threat of anxiety or a breakdown or the threat of a behaviour disorder which makes sense only if the whole be known.

In other words, to those who have more than a certain degree of lack of freedom because of having to cope with the effects of an environmental or perhaps a hereditary failure, health is something which can only be looked at from a distance, and cannot be reached, and those who attain health should be destroyed. The amount of resentment that accumulates in this area is terrific and corresponds to the well person's sense of guilt about being well. In this sense well persons are the 'haves' and the ill people are the 'have-nots'. The well people feverishly organize themselves into giving help to the ill, the unhappy and the unfulfilled, and to those who are liable to commit suicide, just as in the economic sphere those with enough money have the urge to be charitable, as if to keep at bay the flood of resentment expected from the other members of the community who have no food or who lack money which can give them the freedom to move and perhaps to find something worth looking for.

It is impossible to look at the world in more than one way at one time, and although the economic and the psychiatric contrasts have much affinity with each other, nevertheless here one can only draw attention to one aspect of class: that of psychiatric health and ill health. The same subject could be referred to in terms of education or in terms of physical beauty or intelligence quotient. Here it is enough to draw attention to the misunderstanding that must exist between those who are well enough and those who are not well enough in the psychiatric sense. How easy for those who are well enough to develop a kind of smugness, which of course must provoke those who are not well enough into even greater hate.

I am reminded here of a friend of mine, a very fine person, who did a great deal in his medical career and who was very much respected in his private life. He was rather a depressive individual. I remember at a discussion on health he surprised a company of doctors all fully committed to the elimination of disease by starting off his contribution with the words, 'I find health disgusting!' This was serious. He went on (mobilizing his sense of humour) to describe the way in which a friend of his with whom he lived when he was a medical student got up early in the morning and had a cold bath and did exercises and started the day full of glee; he himself, by contrast, was lying in bed in a deep depression, unable to get up except on the basis of a fear of the consequences.

For full consideration of this matter of the psychiatrically ill person's resentment in respect of people who are well enough and not caught up in rigid defences or the symptomatology of an illness, it is necessary to look into the theory of psychiatric disorder. It always seems strange when a psychoanalyst puts stress on the environmental factor. Psychoanalysts of all people have drawn attention to the conflict in the individual that is at the basis of psychoneurosis and of mental disorder. This contribution from psychoanalysis has been of immense value and enabled properly qualified people to do treatment of individuals instead of concentrating on blaming the environment. Individuals like to feel that their illness is their own, and they are relieved to find the analyst trying to seek the roots of their own illness in themselves. To a varying extent, this search is successful. It does matter, however, that the analyst who is doing the treatment is properly selected and is also trained to use the technique, and it helps if he or she is experienced in the work. The environmental factor is therefore not entirely eliminated in any one case. In the search for the aetiology of illness, it has been discovered by the psychoanalysts themselves that one needs to go back to very early matters of the interrelationship between the individual baby or small child and the environment. What Heinz Hartmann referred to as the 'average expectable environment',[2] I myself have referred to as the 'ordinary devoted mother', and others have used similar terms to describe a facilitating environment which must have certain qualities if the maturational processes in the individual child are to take effect and the child is to become a real person in the sense of feeling real in a real world.

Without giving away the tremendous importance of finding the origins of a person's distress in the person and in the person's past history and inner reality, it has become necessary to admit or even to claim that in matters of ultimate aetiology, the important thing is the environment. In other

2. H. Hartmann, *Ego Psychology and the Problem of Adaptation*, New York, International Universities Press, 1939.

words, if the environment is good enough, then the individual baby, small child, growing child, older child and adolescent has the chance to grow according to the potential that is inherited.

On the other side of the line, where the environmental provision is not good enough, the individual, to some degree or perhaps to a high degree, is not capable of reaching to fulfilment of potential. There is therefore a true statement to be made in each case about the haves and the have-nots in psychiatric terms, and one can see resentment operating in terms of this kind of distinction. I am suggesting that while all other kinds of class distinction have validity and produce their own resentments, this one may turn out to be the most significant of all. It is true that a great number of individuals who have done exceptionally well or who have moved the world or who have contributed in an outstanding way have been what they were to the world at great cost, as if they were on the borderline between the haves and the have-nots. One can see how they have made some exceptional contribution out of unhappiness, or been driven by a sense of threat from within. This, however, does not alter the fact that there are two extremes in this area: those who have it in them to fulfil themselves and those who, because of environmental failures in the early stages, are not able to fulfil themselves. It must be expected that the latter resent the existence of the former. The unhappy will try to destroy happiness. Those who are caught up in the prison of the rigidity of their own defences will try to destroy freedom. Those who cannot enjoy their bodies to the full will try to interfere with the enjoyment of the body, even in the case of their own children whom they love. Those who cannot love will try to destroy the simplicity of a natural relationship by cynicism; and (over the border) those who are too ill to take revenge and who spend their lives in mental hospitals make those who are sane feel guilty to be sane and to be free to live in society and to take part in local or world politics.

There are many ways in which one can describe this to

which I am drawing attention, the danger to freedom which freedom generates. Those who are well enough and free enough must be able to endure the triumph which belongs to their state. Yet nothing but luck gave them the chance to be healthy.

Some Thoughts on the Meaning of the Word 'Democracy'

Written for Human Relations, *June 1950*

First of all let me say that I realize I am offering comments on a subject that is outside my own speciality. Sociologists and political scientists may at first resent this impertinence. Yet it seems to me to be valuable for workers to cross the boundaries from time to time, provided that they realize (as I do indeed) that their remarks must inevitably appear naïve to those who know the relevant literature and who are accustomed to a professional language of which the intruder is ignorant.

This word 'democracy' has great importance at the present time. It is used in all sorts of different senses; here are a few:

1. A social system in which the people rule.
2. A social system in which the people choose the leader.
3. A social system in which people choose the government.
4. A social system in which the government allows the people freedom of:
   (*a*) thought and expression of opinion
   (*b*) enterprise
5. A social system which, being on a run of good fortune, can afford to allow individuals freedom of action.

One can study:

1. The etymology of the word.
2. The history of social institutions – Greek, Roman, etc.
3. The use made of the word by various countries and

cultures at the present time – Great Britain, the United States, Russia, etc.

4. The abuse of the word by dictators and others; hood-winking the people, etc.

In any discussion on a term, such as democracy, it is obviously of first importance that a definition should be reached, suitable for the particular type of discussion.

Psychology of the Use of the Term

Is it possible to study the use of this term psychologically? We accept and are accustomed to psychological studies of other difficult terms such as 'normal mind', 'healthy personality', 'individual well adjusted to society', and we expect such studies to prove valuable in so far as they give unconscious emotional factors their full import. One of the tasks of psychology is to study and present the latent ideas that exist in the use of such concepts, not confining attention to obvious or conscious meaning.

An attempt is made here to initiate a psychological study.

Working Definition of the Term

It does seem that an important latent meaning of this term can be found, namely, that a democratic society is 'mature', that is to say, that it has a quality that is allied to the quality of individual maturity which characterizes its healthy members.

Democracy is here defined, therefore, as 'society well adjusted to its *healthy* individual members'. This definition is in accord with the view expressed by R. E. Money-Kyrle.[1]

It is the way people use this term that is important to the psychologist. A psychological study is justified if there is implied in the term the element of *maturity*. The suggestion is that in all uses of the term there can be found to be implied

1. Mental Health Congress, *Bulletin*, 1958.

the idea of maturity or relative maturity, though it is difficult, as all will admit, to define these terms adequately.

Psychiatric Health

In psychiatric terms, the normal or healthy individual can be said to be one who is mature; according to his or her chronological age and social setting there is an appropriate degree of emotional development. (In this argument physical maturity is assumed.)

Psychiatric health is therefore a term without fixed meaning. In the same way the term 'democratic' need not have a fixed meaning. Used by a community, it may mean *the more rather than the less mature in society structure*. In this way one would expect the frozen meaning of the word to be different in Great Britain, the United States and the Soviet Union, and yet to find that the term retains value because of its implying the recognition of maturity as health.

How can one study the emotional development of society? Such a study must be closely related to the study of the individual. The two studies must take place simultaneously.

Democratic Machinery

An attempt must be made to state the accepted qualities of democratic machinery. The machinery must exist for the *election* of leaders by free vote, true secret ballot. The machinery must exist for the people *to get rid of* leaders by secret ballot. The machinery must exist for the *illogical* election and removal of leaders.

The essence of democratic machinery is the free vote (secret ballot). The point of this is that it ensures the freedom of the people to express deep feelings, *apart from conscious thoughts*.[2]

2. In this respect, proportional representation is antidemocratic, even when secret, because it interferes with free expression of *feelings*, and it is only suitable for specialized conditions in which clever and educated people wish for a test of *conscious* opinions.

In the exercise of the secret vote, the whole responsibility for action is taken by the individual, if he is healthy enough to take it. The vote expresses the outcome of the struggle within himself, the external scene having been internalized and so brought into association with the interplay of forces in his own personal inner world. That is to say, the decision as to which way to vote is the expression of a solution of a struggle within himself. The process seems to be somewhat as follows. The external scene, with its many social and political aspects, is made personal for him in the sense that he gradually identifies himself with all the parties to the struggle. This means that he perceives the external scene in terms of his own internal struggle, and he temporarily allows his internal struggle to be waged in terms of the external political scene. This to-and-fro process involves work and takes time, and it is part of democratic machinery to arrange for a period of preparation. A sudden election would produce an acute sense of frustration in the electorate. Each voter's inner world has to be turned into a political arena over a limited period.

If there is doubt about the secrecy of the ballot, the individual, however healthy, can only express by his vote his *reactions*.

Imposed Democratic Machinery

It would be possible to take a community and to impose on it the machinery that belongs to democracy, but this would not be to create a democracy. Someone would be needed to continue to maintain the machinery (for secret ballot, etc.), and also to force the people to accept the results.

Innate Democratic Tendency

A democracy is an achievement, at a point of time, of a limited society, i.e. of a society that has some natural boundary. Of a true democracy (as the term is used today) one can say: *In this society at this time there is sufficient maturity in the emotional development of a sufficient proportion of the individuals that comprise it for there to exist an innate*[3] *tendency towards the creation and re-creation and maintenance of the democratic machinery.*

It would be important to know what proportion of mature individuals is necessary if there is to be an innate democratic tendency. In another way of expressing this, what proportion of antisocial individuals can a society contain without submergence of innate democratic tendency?

Supposition

If the Second World War, and the evacuation scheme in particular, increased the proportion of antisocial children in Great Britain from x per cent to, say, $5x$ per cent, this could easily have affected the education system, so that the educational orientation was towards the $5x$ per cent antisocials, crying out for dictatorship methods, and away from the $100 - 5x$ per cent children who were not antisocial.

A decade later this problem would be stated in this way: that, whereas society could cope with x per cent criminals by segregation of them in prisons, $5x$ per cent of them would tend to produce a general reorientation towards criminals.

Immature Identification with Society

In a society at any one time, if there is x quantity of indivi-

3. By 'innate' I intend to convey the following: the natural tendencies in human nature (hereditary) bud and flower into the democratic way of life (social maturity), but this only happens through the healthy emotional development of individuals; only a proportion of individuals in a social group will have had the luck to develop to maturity, and therefore it is only through them that the innate (inherited) tendency of the group towards social maturity can be implemented.

duals who show their lack of sense of society by developing an antisocial tendency, there is z quantity of individuals reacting to inner insecurity by the alternative tendency – identification with authority. This is unhealthy, immature, because it is not an identification with authority that arises out of self-discovery. It is a sense of frame without sense of picture, a sense of form without retention of spontaneity. This is a prosociety tendency that is anti-individual. People who develop in this way can be called 'hidden antisocials'.

Hidden antisocials are not 'whole persons' any more than are manifest antisocials, since each needs to find and to control the conflicting force in the external world outside the self. By contrast, the healthy person, who is capable of becoming depressed, is able to find the whole conflict within the self as well as being able to see the whole conflict outside the self, in external (shared) reality. When healthy persons come together, they each contribute a whole world, because each brings a whole person.

Hidden antisocials provide material for a type of leadership which is sociologically immature. Moreover, this element in a society greatly strengthens the danger that derives from its frank antisocial elements, especially since ordinary people so easily let those with an urge to lead get into key positions. Once in such positions, these immature leaders immediately gather to themselves the obvious antisocials, who welcome them (the immature anti-individual leaders) as their natural masters. (False resolution of splitting.)

The Indeterminates

It is never as simple as this, because, if there are $(x + z)$ per cent antisocial individuals in a community, it is not true to say that $100 - (x + z)$ per cent are 'social'. There are those in an indeterminate position. One could put it:

Antisocials x per cent

Indeterminates y per cent

Prosociety but anti-individual z per cent

Healthy individuals capable of
   social contribution $100 - (x + y + z)$ per cent

Total   100 per cent

The whole democratic burden falls on the $100 - (x + y + z)$ per cent of individuals who are maturing as individuals, and who are gradually becoming able to add a social sense to their well-grounded personal development.

What percentage does $100 - (x + y + z)$ per cent represent, for instance, in Great Britain today? Possibly it is quite small, say 30 per cent. Perhaps, if there are 30 per cent mature persons, as many as 20 per cent of the indeterminates will be sufficiently influenced to be counted as mature, thus bringing the total to 50 per cent. If, however, the mature percentage should drop to 20, it must be expected that there will be a bigger fall in the percentage of indeterminates able to act in a mature way. If 30 per cent maturity in a community collects 20 per cent indeterminates, i.e. a total of 50 per cent, perhaps 20 per cent maturity in a community collects only 10 per cent indeterminates, i.e. a total of 30 per cent.

Whereas a 50 per cent total might indicate sufficient innate democratic tendency for practical purposes, 30 per cent could not be counted sufficient to avoid submergence by the sum of the antisocials (hidden and manifest) and the indeterminates who would be drawn by weakness or fear into association with them.

There follows an antidemocratic tendency, a tendency towards dictatorship, characterized at first by a feverish bolstering up of the democratic façade (hoodwinking function of the term).

One sign of this tendency is the corrective institution, the localized dictatorship, the practising ground for the personally immature leaders who are reversed antisocials (prosocial but anti-individual).

This, the corrective institution, has both the prison and the mental hospital of a healthy society perilously near to it, and for this reason the doctors of criminals and of the insane have to be constantly on guard lest they find themselves being used, without at first knowing it, as agents of the antidemocratic tendency. There must, in fact, always be a borderline in which there is no clear distinction between the corrective treatment of the political or ideational opponent and the therapy of the insane person. (Here lies the social danger of physical methods of therapy of the mental patient, as compared with true psychotherapy, or even the acceptance of a state of insanity. In psychotherapy the patient is a person on equal terms with the doctor, with a right to be ill, and also a right to claim health and full responsibility for personal, political or ideational views.)

Creation of Innate Democratic Factor

If democracy is maturity, and maturity is health, and health is desirable, then we wish to see whether anything can be done to foster it. Certainly it will not help to impose democratic machinery on a country.

We must turn to the $100 - (x + y + z)$ group of individuals. All depends on them. Members of this group can instigate research.

We find that at any one time we can do nothing to increase the quantity of this innate democratic factor comparable in importance to what has already been done (or not done) by the parents and homes of these individuals when they were infants and children and adolescents.

We can, however, try to avoid compromising the future. We can try to avoid interfering with the homes that can cope, and are actually coping, with their own individual children and adolescents. These *ordinary good homes* provide the only setting in which the innate democratic factor can be created.[4] This is indeed a modest statement of positive contribution, but there is a surprising amount of complexity in its application.

Factors Adverse to the Functioning of the Ordinary Good Home

1. It is very difficult for people to recognize that the essential of a democracy really does lie with the ordinary man and woman, and the ordinary, common-place home.

2. Even if a wise government policy gives parents freedom to run their homes in their own way, it is not certain that officials putting official policies into practice will respect the parents' position.

3. Ordinary good parents do need help. They need all that science can offer in respect of physical health and the prevention and treatment of physical disease; also they want instruction in child care, and help when their children have psychological illnesses or present behaviour problems. But, if they seek such assistance, can they be sure they will not have their responsibilities lifted from them? If this happens they cease to be creators of the innate democratic factor.

4. Many parents are not ordinary good parents. They are psychiatric cases, or they are immature, or they are antisocial in a wide sense, and socialized only in a restricted sense; or they are unmarried, or in unstable relationship, or bickering, or separated from each other, and so on. These parents get attention from society because of their defects. The thing is, can society see that the orientation towards these pathological

---

4. The ordinary good home is something that defies statistical investigation. It has no news value, is not spectacular, and does not produce the men and women whose names are publicly known. My assumption, based on 20,000 case histories taken personally over a period of twenty-five years, is that in the community in which I work the ordinary good home is common, even usual.

features must not be allowed to affect society's orientation towards the ordinary healthy homes?

5. In any case, the parents' attempt to provide a home for their children, in which the children can grow as individuals, and each *gradually add* a capacity to identify with the parents and then with wider groupings, starts at the beginning, when the mother comes to terms with her infant. Here the father is the protecting agent who frees the mother to devote herself to her baby.

The place of the home has long been recognized, and in recent years a great deal has been found out by psychologists as to the ways in which a stable home not only enables children to find themselves and to find each other, but also makes them begin to qualify for membership of society in a wider sense.

This matter of interference with the early infant–mother relationship, however, needs some special consideration. In our society there is increasing interference at this point, and there is extra danger from the fact that some psychologists actually claim that at the beginning it is only physical care that counts. This can only mean that in the unconscious fantasy of people in general, the most awful ideas cluster round the infant–mother relationship. Anxiety in the unconscious is represented in practice by:

1. Overemphasis by physicians and even by psychologists on *physical* processes and health.

2. Various theories that breast feeding is bad, that the baby must be trained as soon as born, that babies should not be handled by their mothers, etc.; and (in the negative) that breast feeding *must* be established, that no training whatever should be given, that babies should never be allowed to cry, etc.

3. Interference with the mother's access to her baby in the first days, and with her first presentation of external reality to the infant. This, after all, is the basis of the new indi-

vidual's capacity eventually to become related to ever-widening external reality, and if the mother's tremendous contribution, *through her being devoted*, is spoilt or prevented, there is no hope that the individual will pass eventually into the $100 - (x + y + z)$ group that alone generates the innate democratic factor.

Development of Subsidiary Themes: Election of Persons

Another essential part of the democratic machinery is that it is a *person* who is elected. There is all the difference in the world between (1) the vote for a person; (2) the vote for a party with a set tendency; and (3) the support of a clear-cut principle by ballot.

1. The election of a person implies that the electors believe in themselves as persons, and therefore believe in the person they nominate or vote for. The person elected has the opportunity to act as a person. As a whole (healthy) person he has the total conflict within, which enables him to get a view, albeit a personal one, of total external situations. He may, of course, belong to a party and be known to have a certain tendency. Nevertheless, he can adapt in a delicate way to changing conditions; if he actually changes his main tendency, he can put himself up for re-election.

2. The election of a party or a group tendency is relatively less mature. It does not require of the electors a trust in a human being. For immature persons, nevertheless, it is the only logical procedure, precisely because an immature person cannot conceive of, or believe in, a truly mature individual. The result of the vote for a party or tendency, for a thing and not a person, is the establishment of a rigid outlook, ill adapted for delicate reactions. This *thing* that is elected cannot be loved or hated, and it is suitable for individuals who have a poorly developed sense of self. It could be said that a system of voting is less democratic, because less mature

(in terms of emotional development of the individual), when the accent is on the vote for the principle or party and not on the vote for the person.

3. Much further removed from anything associated with the word 'democracy' is the ballot on a specific point. There is little of maturity about a referendum (although this can be made to fit in with a mature system on exceptional occasions). As an example of the way in which a referendum is unuseful can be cited the peace ballot between the two world wars in Great Britain. People were asked to answer a specific question ('Are you in favour of peace or war?'). A large number of people abstained from voting because they knew that the question was an unfair one. Of those who voted, a big proportion put their crosses against the word 'peace', although in actual fact, when circumstances rearranged themselves, they were in favour of the war when it came and took part in the fighting. The point is that in this type of questioning, there is only room for the expression of the *conscious* wish. There is no relation between putting one's tick against the word 'peace' in such a ballot and voting for a person who is known to be eager for peace, provided the failure to fight does not mean a lazy abandonment of aspirations and responsibilities and the betrayal of friends.

The same objection applies to much of the Gallup Poll and other questionnaires, even although a great deal of trouble is taken to avoid exactly this pitfall. In any case, a vote on a specific point is a very poor substitute indeed for the vote in favour of a person who, once elected, has a space of time in which he can use his own judgement. The referendum has nothing to do with democracy.

Support of Democratic Tendency: Summary

1. The most valuable support is given in a negative way by organized non-interference with the ordinary good mother–infant relationship, and with the ordinary good home.

2. For more intelligent support, even of this negative kind, much research is needed on the emotional development of the infant and the child of all ages, and also on the psychology of the nursing mother and of the father's function at various stages.

3. The existence of this study shows a belief in the value of education in democratic procedure, which of course can only be given in so far as there is understanding, and can only be usefully given to the emotionally mature or healthy individuals.

4. Another important negative contribution would be the avoidance of attempts to implant democratic machinery on total communities. The result can only be failure, and a setback to true democratic growth. The alternative and valuable action is to support the emotionally mature individuals, however few they may be, and to let time do the rest.

Person – Man or Woman?

The point that has to be considered is whether in the place of the word 'person' there can be put 'man' or 'woman'.

The fact is that the political heads of most countries are men, although women are increasingly used for responsible posts. It can perhaps be assumed that men and women have an equal capacity *qua* men and women; or, the other way round, it would not be possible to say that only men could be suitable for leadership on grounds of intellectual or emotional capacity for the highest political post. Nevertheless, this does not dispose of the problem. It is the psychologist's task to draw attention to the *unconscious* factors which are easily left out of account, even in serious discussions on this sort of subject. The thing that has to be considered is unconscious popular feeling in regard to the man or woman who is elected to the position of political chief. If there is a difference in the fantasy according to whether it be a man or a woman, this cannot be ignored, nor can it be brushed aside by the comment that fantasies ought not to count because they are 'only fantasies'.

In psychoanalytical and allied work it is found that all individuals (men and women) have in reserve a certain fear of WOMAN.[5] Some individuals have this fear to a greater extent than others, but it can be said to be universal. This is quite different from saying that an individual fears a particular woman. This fear of WOMAN is a powerful agent in society structure, and it is responsible for the fact that in very few societies does a woman hold the political reins. It is also responsible for the immense amount of cruelty to women, which can be found in customs that are accepted by almost all civilizations.

The root of this fear of WOMAN is known. It is related to the fact that in the early history of every individual who develops well, and who is sane, and who has been able to find himself, there is a debt to a woman – the woman who was devoted to that individual as an infant, and whose devotion was absolutely essential for that individual's healthy development. The original dependence is not remembered, and therefore the debt is not acknowledged, except in so far as the fear of WOMAN represents the first stage of this acknowledgement.

The foundation of the mental health of the individual is laid down at the very beginning when the mother is simply being devoted to her infant, and when the infant is doubly

---

5. It would be out of place to discuss this here in detail, but the idea can be reached best if approached gradually:

   (i) Fear of the parents of very early childhood.

   (ii) Fear of a combined figure, a woman with male potency included in her powers (witch).

   (iii) Fear of the mother who had absolute power at the beginning of the infant's existence to provide, or to fail to provide, the essentials for the early establishment of the self as an individual.

[See also 'The Mother's Contribution to Society' and 'This Feminism' in this volume – Eds.]

dependent because totally unaware of dependence. There is no relation to the father which has such a quality, and for this reason a man who in a political sense is at the top can be appreciated by the group much more objectively than a woman can be if she is in a similar position.

Women often claim that if women were in charge of affairs, there would be no wars. There are reasons why this may be doubted as a final statement of truth, but, even if the claim were justified, it would still not follow that men or women would ever tolerate the general principle of women generally at the highest point of political power. (The Crown, by being outside or beyond politics, is not affected by these considerations.)

As an offshoot of this consideration, one can consider the psychology of the dictator, who is at the opposite pole to anything that the word 'democracy' can mean. *One of the roots of the need to be a dictator can be a compulsion to deal with this fear of woman by encompassing her and acting for her.* The dictator's curious habit of demanding not only absolute obedience and absolute dependence but also 'love' can be derived from this source.

Moreover, the tendency of groups of people to accept or even seek *actual* domination is derived from a fear of domination by *fantasy woman*. This fear leads them to seek, and even welcome, domination by a known human being, especially one who has taken on himself the burden of personifying and therefore limiting the magical qualities of the allpowerful woman of fantasy, to whom is owed the great debt. The dictator can be overthrown, and must eventually die; but the woman figure of primitive unconscious fantasy has no limits to her existence or power.

Child–Parent Relationship

The democratic set-up includes the provision of a certain degree of stability for the elected rulers; as long as they can manage their job without alienating the support of their electors, they carry on. In this way the people arrange for a certain amount of stability which they could not maintain through direct voting on every point, even if that were possible. The psychological consideration here is that there is in the history of every individual the fact of the parent–child relationship. Although in the mature democratic way of political life the electors are presumably mature human beings, it cannot be assumed that there is no place for a residue of the parent–child relationship, with its obvious advantages. To some extent in the democratic election mature people elect temporary parents, which means that they also acknowledge the fact that to some extent the electors remain children. Even the elected temporary parents, the rulers of the democratic political system, are children themselves outside their professional political work. If in driving their cars they exceed the speed limit, they come under ordinary judicial censure, because driving a car is not part of their job of ruling. As political leaders, and only as such, they are temporarily parents, and after being deposed at an election they revert to being children. It is as if it is convenient to play a game of parents and children because things work out better that way. In other words, because there are advantages in the parent–child relationship, some of this is retained; but, for this to be possible, a sufficient proportion of individuals need to be grown-up enough not to mind playing at being children.

In the same way it is thought to be bad for these people who are playing at parents to have no parents themselves. In the game it is generally thought that there should be another house of representatives to which the rulers who are directly elected by the people should be responsible. In this country this function belongs to the House of Lords, which is to some extent composed of those who have a hereditary title, and to some extent of those who have won a position there by eminence in various branches of public work. Once again the 'parents' of the 'parents' are persons, and capable of making positive contributions as human beings. And it makes sense to love or to hate or to respect or to despise persons. There can be no substitute in a society for the human beings or being at the top, in so far as that society is to be rated according to its quality of emotional maturity.

And further, in a study of the social setting in Great Britain, we can see that the lords are children, relative to the Crown. Here in each case we come again to a person, who holds his or her position by heredity, and also by maintaining the love of the people by his or her personality and actions. It is certainly helpful when the reigning monarch quite easily and sincerely carries the matter a stage further and proclaims a belief in God. Here we reach the interrelated subjects of The Dying God and The Eternal Monarch.

Geographical Boundary of a Democracy

For the development of a democracy, in the sense of a mature society structure, it seems that it is necessary that there should be some natural geographical boundary for that society. Obviously, up to recently and even now, the fact that Great Britain is seabound (except for its relation to Eire) has been very much responsible for the maturity of our society structure. Switzerland has (less satisfactorily) mountain limits. America till recently had the advantage of a west which offered unlimited exploitation; this meant that the United States, while being united by positive ties, did not till recently need to start to feel to the full the internal struggles of a closed community, united in spite of hate as well as because of love.

A state that has no natural frontier cannot relax an active adaptation to neighbours. In one sense, fear *simplifies* the emotional situation, for many of the indeterminate y and some of the less severe of the antisocial x become able to identify with the state on the basis of a cohesive reaction to an external persecution threat. This simplification is detrimental, however, to the development towards maturity, which is a difficult thing, involving full acknowledgement of essential conflict, and the non-employment of any way out or way round (defences).

In any case, the basis for a society is the whole human personality, and the personality has a limit. The diagram of a healthy person is a circle (sphere), so that whatever is not-self can be described as either inside or outside that person. It is not possible for persons to get further in society-building than they can get with their own personal development.

For these reasons we regard with suspicion the use of terms like 'world-citizenship'. Perhaps only a few really great and fairly aged men and women ever get as far in their own development as to be justified in thinking in such wide terms.

If the whole world were our society, then it would need to be at times in a depressed mood (as a person at times inevitably has to be), and it would have to be able fully to acknowledge essential conflict within itself. The concept of a global society brings with it the idea of the world's suicide, as well as the idea of the world's happiness. For this reason we expect the militant protagonists of the world state to be individuals who are in a manic swing of a manic-depressive psychosis.

Education in Democratic Lore

Such democratic tendency as exists can be strengthened by a study of the psychology of social, as well as of individual, maturity. The results of such study must be given in understandable language to the existing democracies and to healthy individuals everywhere, so that they may become *intelligently self-conscious*. Unless they are self-conscious they cannot know what to attack and what to defend, nor can they recognize threats to democracy when these arise. 'The price of freedom is eternal vigilance': vigilance by whom? – by two or three of the $100 - (x + y + z)$ per cent mature individuals. The others are busy just being ordinary good parents, handing on the job of growing up, and of being grown-up, to their children.

Democracy at War

The question must be asked, is there such a thing as democracy at war? The answer is certainly not a plain 'yes'. In fact, there are some reasons why, in war-time, there should be an announcement of temporary suspension of democracy because of war.

It is clear that mature healthy individuals, collectively forming a democracy, should be able to go to war: (1) to make room to grow; (2) to defend what is valued, already possessed, etc.; and (3) to fight antidemocratic tendencies in so far as there are people to support such tendencies by fighting.[6]

Nevertheless, it must be but seldom that things have worked out that way. According to the description given above, a community is never composed of 100 per cent of healthy, mature individuals.

As soon as war approaches, there is a rearrangement of groups, so that by the time war is being fought it is not the healthy who are doing all the fighting. Taking our four groups:

1. Many of the antisocials, along with mild paranoiacs, feel better because of actual war, and they welcome the real persecution threat. They find a prosocial tendency by active fighting.

2. Of the indeterminates, many step over into what is the thing to do, perhaps using the grim reality of war to grow up as they would not otherwise have done.

3. Of the hidden antisocials, probably some find opportunity for the urge to dominate in the various key positions which war creates.

4. The mature, healthy individuals do not necessarily show up as well as the others. They are not so certain as the others are that the enemy is bad. They have doubts. Also, they have a bigger positive stake in the world's culture, and in beauty

6. A fuller statement of these ideas will be found in 'Discussion of War Aims' in this volume. [Eds.]

and in friendship, and they cannot easily believe war is necessary. Compared with the near-paranoiacs, they are slow in getting the gun in hand and in pulling the trigger. In fact, they miss the bus to the front line, even if when they get there they are the reliable factor and the ones best able to adapt to adversity.

Moreover, some of the healthy of peace-time become anti-social in war (conscientious objectors), not from cowardice but from a genuine personal doubt, just as the antisocials of peace-time tend to find themselves in brave action in war.

For these and other reasons, when a democratic society is fighting, it is the whole group that fights, and it would be difficult to find an instance of a war conducted by just those of a community who provide the innate democratic factor in peace.

It may be that when a war has disturbed a democracy, it is best to say that at that moment democracy is at an end, and those who like that way of life will have to start again and fight inside the group for the re-establishment of democratic machinery, after the end of the external conflict.

This is a large subject, and it deserves the attention of large-minded people.

Summary

1. The use of the word 'democracy' can be studied psychologically on the basis of its implication of maturity.

2. Neither democracy nor maturity can be implanted on a society.

3. Democracy is an achievement of a limited society at any one time.

4. The innate democratic factor in a community derives from the workings of the ordinary good home.

5. The main activity for promotion of democratic tendency is a negative one: avoidance of interference with the ordinary good home. Study of psychology and education according to what is known provides additional help.

6. There is special significance in the devotion of the ordinary good mother to her infant, the capacity for eventual emotional maturity being founded as a result of the devotion. Mass interference at this point, in a society, would quickly and effectually lessen the democratic potential of that society, just as it would diminish the richness of its culture.

The Place of the Monarchy

Written in 1970

I propose to look at the place of the monarchy in Great Britain. I have to do this without specialized knowledge of the literature specifically relating to the monarchy, and without specialization in history, but the excuse is perhaps a valid one that the monarchy is something that we live with, and we all the time keep ourselves informed through seeing what appears on television, in the popular press, and through conversations with taxi drivers and with friends at the local. I happen to live quite near the flag over Buckingham Palace, which shows, by its flying or its being folded, whether the Queen is or is not resident; but for everyone in this country at the present time, there is a permanent and vital question: has God saved the Queen? Behind this is the saying, 'The King is dead, long live the King!', which is significant in that it implies that the monarchy survives the death of the reigning monarch. Here is the crux of the matter.

It will be observed already that although I am not unduly sentimental about royalty and royal families, I do nevertheless take the existence of the monarchy seriously, believing that without the monarchy Great Britain would be quite a different place to live in, leaving aside the other question: would some alternative be better or worse? And also leaving aside all the complex considerations that belong to an objective assessment of what today's king or queen is really like, as a person.

As a preliminary to the making of an examination of the

monarchy and its place in the community, it is natural to ask the question: what do ordinary people say if they are properly approached and given the chance to express a personal opinion? Of course, most people have two sets of attitudes: a feeling attitude and a conversational attitude.

The conversational attitude is the one that is expressed in the game called talking. Verbalization gives us scope for a wide exploration of possibilities, and in discussion we may hold opposing views at one and the same time, and we may simply argue for pleasure. In this kind of attitude-display, which has great value, it is nevertheless true that most people ignore the awful complication of unconscious motivation. The unconscious is thought of as a nuisance, something that spoils the fun. The unconscious belongs to psychoanalysis and the therapy of ill people. In the pub let us say what we think we know and give rationalizations that pass for reasons. And let us not be too serious, else we find ourselves in love or at war before we have time to say Jack Robinson. Yet serious conversation is evidence of civilization, and talkers must be invited to allow for the unconscious. The feeling attitude, being a total response, does include the unconscious; but people cannot immediately do justice to their feelings as whole people.

In the verbalized attitude towards the monarchy's place in our culture, we find that the whole business of royalty is only too easily treated as a fairy tale. It may be that the fairy tale is felt to be cosy, happy-making, an enrichment of daily living. Or it may be that the fairy tale is felt to be an escapist exercise, weakening our resolve to alter bad things in the economy, bad or inadequate housing, the loneliness of old people, the helplessness of the physically handicapped, the discomfort of squalor and poverty, or the tragedy of persecutions based on prejudice. The word 'escapist' sums up this attitude, and on these grounds the fairy tale is already damned.

Corresponding to this is the word 'sentimental', which belongs to the attitude of those who do not ever really quite wake up, who fail to see the awfulness of a slum and who have already withdrawn into make-believe.

Those who use the word 'escapist' despise those who are sentimental; the sentimental do not exactly know what to do with their opposite numbers, until they find themselves, bewildered, mixed up in a political situation, perhaps a revolution that has no meaning for them.

Unconscious Use of the Monarchy

The assumption underlying what I am discussing here is itself difficult to understand or assume. It goes right to the base of the existence of the human individual, and to the most fundamental aspect of object-relating. The axiom is: *What is good is always being destroyed*. This involves the concept of unconscious intention. Its truth is somewhat similar to the truth in the saying, 'Beauty is in the eye of the beholder.'[1]

This is one of the facts of life. It appears immediately in our national anthem, 'God Save the Queen/King!' Save from what? It is too easy to think of saving the King or Queen from enemies, although full justice is done to this idea in the later lines of the anthem. ('Their knavish tricks' is great fun, but we know that this is not the hub of the matter.) What human beings cannot leave alone is something good. They must get it and destroy it.

Survival Apart from Preservation

It is a pertinent question: why does any good thing exist if the fact of its existence and of its goodness incites people and may lead to its destruction? There is an answer, an answer that calls on the actual qualities of the good thing. The good thing *may survive*. Survival may be a fact because of properties of the good thing that is always being destroyed. Then

1. Winnicott's main statement of the ideas expressed here is to be found in 'The Use of an Object', in *Playing and Reality*, London, Tavistock Publications, 1971; New York, Basic Books, 1971; Harmondsworth, Penguin Books, 1985. [Eds.]

the good thing is loved, valued and almost worshipped in a new way. It has come through the test of being ruthlessly used and of having been the object, unprotected by us, of our most primitive impulses and ideas.

The monarchy is always under test. It may survive over difficult phases because of royalist or loyalist support, but in the end everything depends on the kings and the queens who find themselves, apart from personal choice, on the throne, in king-position.

This is where the heredity principle comes into its own. This man (or woman) is not on the throne because of choice, his choice or our choice, or because of a political vote, or because of merit, but because of heredity.

Looking at the matter this way, we find it to be almost a miracle that the monarchy has survived in our country for more than a thousand years. There have been precarious moments, failures in the provision of heirs, unloved or unloveable persons placed willy-nilly in the king-position, and there have been king-deaths. But cessation of the monarchy has been a rare phenomenon, so much so that we immediately think of Cromwell, who perhaps helped the country to see that a good dictator can be worse than a bad king.

There are two major considerations that arise out of the fact of the survival of a good thing that has been subjected to the full range of feeling without protection, which implies inhibition of impulse and a postponement of the moment of truth, the real test.

One of these considerations concerns the individuals involved at any one time. The survival of the thing (here, monarchy) makes it valuable, and enables people of all kinds and ages to see that the will to destruction had nothing to do with anger – it had to do with love of a primitive kind, and the destruction occurs in the unconscious fantasy, or in the personal dream that belongs to being asleep. It is in the personal inner psychic reality that the thing is destroyed. In waking life, survival of the object, whatever it is, brings a sense of relief and a new sense of confidence. It is now clear that *because of their own properties* things can survive, in spite of our dream, in spite of the backcloth of destruction in our unconscious fantasy. The world now begins to exist as a place in its own right; a place to live in, not as a place to fear or to be complied with or to be lost in, or to be dealt with only in day-dream or fantasy-indulgence.

Much of the violence in the world belongs to an attempt to reach the destruction that is in itself not destructive, unless, of course, the object fails to survive, or becomes provoked into retaliation. There is therefore a profound and a great value to the individual in the survival of central things, of which in our country the monarchy is one. Reality becomes more real and the personal impulse of primitive exploration less dangerous.

The other consideration has to do with politics. In a country that is not too big and that has a history and if possible is an island (no frontiers, except the sea itself), it is possible to keep up a duality, a political system with the government periodically liable to be turned out, and the monarchy indestructible ('The King is dead, long live the King').

It is obvious, and yet needs restatement from time to time, that the working of the democratic parliamentary system (opposed in idea to dictatorship) depends on the survival of the monarchy, and *pari passu* the survival of the monarchy depends on the people's feeling that they really can, by voting, turn a government out in a parliamentary election or get rid of a prime minister. It is assumed here that the turning out of a government or a prime minister must be on the basis of feeling, as expressed in secret ballot, and not on a basis of the poll (Gallup and other) that fails to give expression to deep feeling or to unconscious motivation or to trends that seem illogical.

The riddance of a political figure or party involves a less immediate thing, namely, the election of an alternative political head. In the case of the monarchy itself, this is solved in advance. In this way a monarchy can give rise to a feeling of stability in a country where the political scene is in a state of turmoil, as periodically it should be.

The Place of the Person in King-Position

It is fortunately true that the survival of the monarchy does not depend on psychology or on logical understanding, or on a clever word to be uttered by a philosopher or a religious leader. Survival in the end depends on the man or woman who is on the throne. It could be interesting to look into the theory that could be built around these highly significant phenomena.

All the time we are conscious of the fact that whereas a monarchy can be founded on a thousand years of history, it could be destroyed in a day. It could be destroyed by false theory or by irresponsible journalism. It could be laughed out of existence by those who only see a fairy story or who see a ballet or a play when really they are looking at an aspect of life itself. This aspect of life itself needs to be spelt out clearly, because of its not generally being allowed for in descriptive talk. It concerns the intermediate area where the transitions from the sleeping to the waking and from waking to sleeping take place. This is the place for play and cultural experience, and the place that is occupied by transitional objects, and transitional phenomena, all evidences of personal psychiatric health.[2]

Surprisingly, although the theory of human personality and living is chiefly described in terms of the alternatives of personal dream and actual or shared reality, when we look without blinkers we see that most of the life of adults, adolescents, children, and small children and babies is spent in this intermediate area. Civilization itself can be described in these terms.

2. See *Playing and Reality*, London Tavistock Publications, 1971; New York, Basic Books, 1971; Harmondsworth, Penguin Books, 1985, and in particular Chapter 1, 'Transitional Objects and Transitional Phenomena'. [Eds.].

The study of the area is best made first in terms of babies living in the care of good-enough mothers and fathers with adequate home life. I have stated as clearly as I am able to that the characteristic of this area of transitional phenomena is *the acceptance of the paradox* that links external reality to inner experience. This is the paradox that must never be resolved. In terms of the baby with a piece of cloth or a teddy-bear essential for security and happiness and symbolic of an ever-available mother or mother-element (or father-element), we never make the challenge: did you create this or did you find something already there? The *answer* is not significant, although the *question* is relevant and significant.

In terms of the monarchy, the man or woman who is on the throne is everyone's dream *and yet* is a real man or woman with all human characteristics.

Only if we are remote from this woman, the Queen, can we afford to dream and to place her in the area of myth. If we live in close proximity, presumably we find it difficult to maintain the dream. For the millions, and I am one of these millions, this woman is acting my dream for me and at the same time she is a human being whom I might see in her car as I sit waiting in a taxi while she emerges from Buckingham Palace to perform some function which is part of her living out the role assigned to her by fate, and in which she is maintained by most of us. While I am cursing because of the delay which means that I shall be late for my appointment, I know that we need the formality, the deference, and the dream-come-true paraphernalia. Quite possibly the woman who is queen is sometimes hating it all too, but *we never know*, because we have nearly no access to the details of this particular woman's life and person, this being the way to keep up her dream-significance. Without her dream-significance, she is only a neighbour.

Of course we shall try to pull aside the veils. We enjoy reading about Queen Victoria, and we invent stories both sentimental and scurrilous, but in the centre of it all is a woman (or man) who has or has not the capacity to survive, to exist without reacting to provocation or to seduction, until at death a successor determined by heredity takes over this terrible responsibility. It is a terrible responsibility, because it is unreal in its stark reality, because where there is life there can be death, because at the crucial moment there is isolation, a degree of aloneness that is unparalleled.

In examining this intermediate area where we live and play, where we are creative, the paradox must be tolerated, not resolved. To make this point clearer, the fact of the royal pictures could be examined. These, which have immense artistic value, have been collected by the Queen and her ancestors over the centuries, and they belong to her. Yet at the same time, they belong to the nation – to each one of us – because the Queen is our queen and is the embodiment of our dream. Imagine the liquidation of the monarchy, and immediately this collection of lovely things becomes a list of priced goods in a catalogue, and we have lost it all to whomsoever happens to have pounds or dollars to spare at a specific moment.

As it is, with the Queen representing us in ownership, we do not need to think at all in false terms of cash value.

Summary

The survival of the monarchy depends, therefore, on its own inherent qualities; its place alongside the political wrangle in parliament and at the hustings, which is largely conducted in verbal form; its dependence on our own dream or total unconscious potential; its dependence on what the woman (or man) in king-position is actually like, and on the nature of the royal family, and on chance matters of life and death because of accident and disease; on the general psychiatric health of the community, comprised of a not too big proportion of persons resentful because of deprivation, or ill because of privations in earliest relationships; on geographical factors; and so on.

It would be a mistaken idea to think that we ourselves will

preserve what we feel to be good. In the end it must be the survival capacity of the actual monarch that settles the issue. At present we seem to be fortunate. We may deeply appreciate the strain that goes with the great honour and privilege of being on the throne of this country, a country which is not too big, and which has sea around it, and which once had a song about it: 'A Nice Little Tight Little Island'.

Conclusion

My thesis is that it is not a matter of saving the monarchy. It is the other way round. The continued existence of the monarchy is one of the indications we have that there exist here and now the conditions in which democracy (a reflection of family affairs in a social setting) can characterize the political system, and in which a benign or a malignant dictatorship (and each of these is based on fear) is for the time being unlikely to appear. Under such conditions, individuals, if they are emotionally healthy, can develop a sense of being, can realize some of their personal potential, and can play.

Index